THE OWNER'S COMPREHENSIVE GUIDE TO
TRAINING AND SHOWING
YOUR HORSE

MARIE CAHILL

THE OWNER'S COMPREHENSIVE GUIDE TO
TRAINING AND SHOWING
YOUR HORSE

MARIE CAHILL

MALLARD
PRESS

First published in the United States of America
in 1991 by The Mallard Press
Mallard Press and its accompanying design
and logo are trademarks of BDD Promotional
Book Company, Inc.

ISBN 0-7924-5594-0

Printed in Hong Kong

Designed by Ruth DeJauregui

ACKNOWLEDGEMENTS
The author would like to thank Kathy Fallon of
the American Horse Shows Association for
reading the manuscript; Sarah Cohen for her
guidance; Steve Sloan for his inspiration; and
Deborah Young for her assistance.

Page 1: Lacey Bailey and her friend,
Remington Steele. This prize-winning
horse, owned by Patti Bailey, is the epi-
tome of Arabian type with long legs and
neck, and a vibrant personality.
Pages 2-3: Morgans grazing at the Morgan Horse Ranch at Point Reyes National
Seashore in California.
This page, top: To ensure top performance, feeding time comes *after* the
show. *This page, bottom:* Horse and
handler watch an event while they wait
for their turn in the ring.

CONTENTS

TRAINING YOUR HORSE

Above: **A pony goes through his paces for the judge in a beginner's dressage class.**

Facing page: **Getting acquainted is the first step in training a horse.**

The best, most effective way to train any animal is to understand its natural instincts. By understanding what motivates an animal, you will have a better idea of how it will react when you introduce it to a new concept. Horses are motivated by fear and the herd instinct.

Horses fear the unknown. The training process must be slow so that the horse is given plenty of time to evaluate the situation. It's only natural for your horse to be frightened the first time a saddle is placed on his back. Therefore, a horse must be taught not to fear the saddle before it is ever placed on his back.

In the wild, horses do not live alone; they exist in herds and, to a large extent, their behavior is governed by the mood of the herd. The herd instinct can be a helpful training tool, especially when you advance to cross-country riding. A young horse will not be as frightened by objects along the trail if he is with older, quiet horses.

Though all horses need to learn the basics, as training progresses it becomes extremely particular. To the novice horse trainer, the possibilities are endless. Horses can be trained for dressage, for hunting, for competitive trail riding and so on.

TRAINING A YOUNG FOAL

GETTING ACQUAINTED.

The first step in training a foal is getting acquainted. Before you ever introduce your foal to a halter you need to accustom him to being handled. Your goal is to teach him not to fear being restrained. This is accomplished by encircling your arms around his entire body. Be gentle but firm, placing one arm around the chest and the other the hindquarters. The foal will struggle to be released. Quiet the foal down by speaking to him in a soft voice, releasing him only

Above: **Your horse's earliest lessons— halter training, leading, learning to stand—provide an essential base for showing your horse when he matures. Once he reaches the show ring, he will have learned to stand by your side or to wait calmly when he is tied up.**

when he calms down. Your foal has just learned a most important lesson—no harm will come to him even though he was restrained. Repeat the procedure several times. Gradually the foal will allow you to flex his head and neck without him stiffening his muscles. If you use this method on a very young foal—one that is only a few days old—halter training will be much easier.

Getting acquainted is the first step regardless of the horse's age. Even if you purchase a three- or four-year-old that has already been trained by someone else, you and your horse will want to spend some time just getting to know one another.

HALTER TRAINING. When your foal is about two weeks old, begin halter training. The first halter training lesson reinforces the getting acquainted 'lesson' he learned earlier. You want him to be submissive when restrained. It is not yet time to lead him. Place the halter on the foal's head and adjust it so that its fits well but not too tightly. Attach a lead rope to the halter and allow the foal to test it. As he moves his head he will feel a strange pressure, which will naturally frighten him. Hold the lead firmly and let the foal discover for himself that the pressure stops when he stops pulling and jerking. If he has learned his first lesson well, he will cease to struggle fairly soon.

Halter training an older foal, whether he is two months or two years, is more difficult simply by virtue of his size and strength. If he is too strong for you to hold securely, you may have to tie him to a post. Some trainers recommend tying the foal to a heavy duty rubber inner tube that is secured to the post instead of tying him directly to the post. The tube is flexible but will not break. Others like to use a rope halter with sheepskin padding over the crownpiece and noseband. Whatever method you use, make sure the foal cannot break free. If he breaks away before he becomes accustomed to the halter, he learns that a struggle may set him loose—and that is the exact opposite of what you are trying to teach him. Once having broken free, he may be tempted to struggle every time the halter is placed on him. You run the risk of having created a halter-puller.

Placing a halter on an older foal may pose its share of problems. If the foal is fearful of being handled, you will need to take things one step at a time. The first step is to let him become accustomed to you. Begin by simply bringing his food and water into the paddock, calmly standing nearby as he eats. Spend time with him in the paddock so that he does not feel threatened. Eventually, he will eat grain out of a pail in your hand and will allow you to stroke his neck. That accomplished you will be able to place the halter on his head. Then use the pail of grain to lead him to the post where you plan to tie him. Have the lead rope already securely in place. Snap the rope to the halter and move out of the way as the foal will begin to struggle as soon as he feels the rope tighten.

There is no way to determine how long an older foal will fight being tied. Stand back and let him struggle without interference. Once the foal has calmed down leave him tied to the post, perhaps for as long as an hour. If the foal starts to paw the ground, ignore him rather than shouting at him or punishing him. Attention of any sort will only serve to reinforce the undesirable behavior.

After the tying lesson is over, remove the halter from the horse. He may harm himself by snagging the halter on something. Horses have been known to catch a forefoot in a halter by stepping into it while grazing or by reaching forward with a hind foot to scratch the jaw.

LEADING. With a very young foal that is still with his mother, you can conduct your first leading lesson with the mare's assistance. Begin by leading him alongside the mare, then halt him and allow the mare to continue on a short distance. You will need a helper to lead the mare. The foal may attempt to follow his mother. If so, wait until he calms down and then lead him to the mare.

Wait a day so that this latest lesson will sink in and begin to lead him the next day. If you are training a foal that is only two weeks you may want to wait even longer. New lessons are always somewhat upsetting, especially for such a young animal.

To make this task a little easier, loop a soft rope around his hindquarters, just above the hocks. By tugging on the hindquarters rope and pulling on the halter rope, you should be able to coax him along. After the foal has followed you and settled down, lead the mare to him.

To lead an older foal, tighten the lead line just enough to apply pressure. Do not pull on the line. Pulling only encourages the horse to pull the other way. Instead, think of yourself as a post to which the foal is tied; your job is to *resist* the foal's struggles. If your foal has learned his first lesson, he will not struggle. He should step forward to slacken the pressure from the lead line. This is exactly what you want him to do. Leave the rope slack for a minute so that he will understand that he did the right thing. Then tighten the line again to encourage him to take another step forward. Continue the process of pausing and making the line taut. Progress will be slow and tedious but the foal should catch on that you want him to follow. Use voice commands to help you coax him along.

Of course, not all horses will catch on as quickly. You may have to resort to a hindquarters loop, as for a young foal. Another alternative is to have a friend, from a safe distance behind the horse, shoo the horse ahead. Your goal for this introductory lesson is to teach the horse to walk forward and follow you in response to a signal of pressure on the lead line. At this point, you are concerned with leading at its most basic. You can walk with the foal behind you and later you can work on teaching him to walk alongside you.

TEACHING A HORSE TO STAND. While working on leading, you can also work on teaching your horse good manners. In other words, you want to have a horse that is well behaved, whether he is tied at halter or being groomed. Teaching your horse to stand quietly should be a fairly easy lesson for him to learn. Every day for about two weeks, tie your horse in the stable yard for two to three hours. You can keep him tied while you busy yourself with other tasks around the stable, but be sure to keep him tied for at least two hours. Your horse must learn that standing and waiting may last awhile. He'll accept the lesson much more readily if there is activity nearby—other horses or other people. If you plan to compete in horse

Above: **Before you introduce your horse to a halter he must readily accept being handled, otherwise he will struggle and try to pull away when you put the halter on him. Note that the trainer holds a crop, which he will use to encourage the horse to move if he doesn't follow his voice commands.**

shows, the time spent teaching your horse to stand patiently will prove to be time well spent.

HANDLING YOUR FOAL. At this stage, your foal must also learn that you mean him no harm. He must learn to accept handling without feeling frightened. He also needs to learn not to be frightened by anything that might brush against him on a trail–a leaf falling from a tree or a branch.

To accustom your foal to being handled, gently rub your hands all over him. While the foal is standing quietly, massage the foal from the shoulder to the knee and from the knee to the fetlock, pressing with your index finger and thumb. Pick up the foot and hold it for a few minutes. Next massage the head and neck and then move down the back, over the hips, down the flank, across the stifle to the buttocks. Continue down to the hock and the fetlock. Pick up his hind leg and hold it for a moment. Be sure to repeat the process on both sides of the foal.

The foal will probably fidget while you are handling him, but if he starts to crowd you he is becoming aggressive and may lash out with his legs. Always be in tune with your horse's mood so you can step back if the need arises.

Some trainers use an old method called sacking. In recent years, sacking has become the object of controversy because some people

believe that it breaks the horse's spirit or humiliates him. However, experienced horse trainers use sacking because it helps a horse overcome his instinctive fear of being touched. The horse submits to handling because he has gained confidence and knows no harm will come to him, and not because he has been broken into submission. The key is that the process is done correctly.

In sacking a horse, the trainer rubs and rustles a large piece of cloth around and over and under a skittish young horse until the horse relaxes and accepts it without fear. The entire process may take an hour or even longer. Some trainers prefer to spend several days sacking a horse.

Rather than having the horse tied to a post, it is better to have him in a paddock and hold him with the halter line in one hand and the cloth in one hand. That way if the horse breaks loose, he won't be able to run very far.

Sacking will make the horse anxious at first—and that is the point of the exercise. The horse has to learn to accept something that makes him feel slightly uneasy. The process must be done slowly and carefully, with trainer remaining calm and reassuring throughout. The most important thing about sacking is that you are in tune with your horse. Watch your horse, and when he is comfortable move onto the next step. The steps described below assume that you are working with a two-year-old horse.

Above: **Stretching the horse's neck by turning the head to each side is a good way to warm-up before riding. Longeing is also a good technique for warming up.**

Above: **A horse that is kept in a stall needs to be exercised and ridden daily. Once you have a established a routine, your horse will look forward to your daily visits.**

Begin with the lead rope in the left hand and the cloth in the right. Some horses will be frightened by the sight of the cloth. Stand several feet away from the horse and hold the cloth so the horse can take a good long look at it. As soon as he seems bored by the cloth, let him examine the cloth if he chooses. Do not pull the cloth away. If the horse starts to back away, walk with him so that the line remains slack.

When the horse stops backing away, encourage him to take a closer look at the cloth. You can expect the horse to feel uneasy, but do not let him become panicky. When the horse relaxes, lower the sack to your side. After a few minutes, raise the cloth again and let the horse take another look at it. Do this a few times, always lowering the cloth when he calms down. He will begin to learn that acting unruly serves no purpose. Once the horse is used to your raising and lowering the cloth, you can try waving it gently through the air. If the action frightens him, return to raising and lowering the cloth a few more times. Then try waving the cloth again.

Once your horse has become accustomed to the cloth, your next objective is to touch the cloth to the side of his neck, near the shoulder and hold it there. To do this, take a step toward the horse, lifting the cloth with a smooth, easy motion. You need to be confident. If you are nervous, the horse will sense your mood and be nervous, too.

Talking to the horse in a soothing voice will help to calm him down and to reassure him. He learns to respond to your voice and this is useful when you encounter something scary around the stable, on the trail or while doing any kind of trail or jumping course.

Many horses feel startled by the touch of the cloth and will pull away—a reaction that trainers tend to mirror involuntarily. Keep the horse from panicking. Ease the cloth away slightly but do not pull the cloth away quickly. Lower the cloth only when the horse calms down. He is learning that there is nothing to fear from the cloth.

Once the horse has become used to the feel of the cloth, you can begin to rub his neck and then the shoulders. Remember to watch your horse for his reaction. Don't be too quick with the cloth. Throughout the entire process, keep the lead line loose, as a tight line will give the horse a feeling a being trapped.

When your horse becomes totally unconcerned about the cloth, be a little bolder with the cloth and *gently* swing it against his shoulder. The horse may shy away from the cloth. His natural instincts tell him to run from what he fears, so reassure him by reminding him of what he already knows about the cloth. The cloth did not harm him when you rubbed it against him. Rub the cloth against his shoulder and then try swinging it against him. You may want to alternate a rub with a swing. When the swinging cloth against his shoulder is no longer disturbing to your horse, very slowly begin to swing it gently against the body and then the legs. The swinging cloth should *never* sting the horse, for that would undermine your purpose. Sacking teaches your horse there is nothing to fear.

When your horse has grown accustomed to the swinging cloth, rub the cloth behind his ears and under his jaw. After you have handled his head, tie him up and sack him on the hindquarters.

All horses will react somewhat differently to being sacked, but all will share a fear of the sacking cloth and most horses will respond by trying to get away from the cloth. Though extremely rare, a horse may react by lashing out with his forelegs and rearing up on his back. In a case like this, the trainer should end the sacking immediately. Although sacking an aggressive horse can be effective, safety precautions, such as a humane hobbler, are called for, and the novice trainer should seek the help of an experienced trainer.

CONTROLLING YOUR HORSE FROM A DISTANCE

Above: Longeing is a useful technique for training as well as daily exercise. You can use either a rope or longe line, made of cotton or nylon webbing.

Longeing is a useful technique for training a young horse. Up to this point, your primary concern has been teaching your horse to accept handling. Longeing teaches discipline. In longeing the horse will learn to respond to commands to perform certain maneuvers. He will learn to walk, trot and canter for as long as required, providing the basis for saddle training.

Longeing also lays the foundation for schooling in collection and jumping, both of which can be introduced with the longe line. An added benefit of longeing is that it allows you to exercise your horse when you are not planning to go riding.

For longeing, you will need the following equipment: a longe line and a whip. The line is about 25 feet long; the whip has a stock about five to six feet long, while the lash is eight to ten feet long. Both items are made specifically for longeing.

Your first lesson should take place in an enclosed area. A paddock only slightly larger than the maximum size of the longeing circle is the ideal size. Even though your horse is on a line, it is a good idea to work in an enclosed area. If the horse becomes entangled in the rope, you will have to release the line. The enclosure also works as a training aid, with the walls reinforcing the notion that the horse must move in a circle.

Before beginning the first lesson, introduce the horse to the whip, letting him examine it closely. He needs to know there is nothing to fear, so gradually rub the whip against him and wave it through the air. A whip is an effective tool because it lengthens a trainer's arm. It guides the horse, urging him forward or checking him, as need be.

THE FIRST LONGEING LESSON. Keep the first session short, no more than 10 minutes. If the task becomes unpleasant for the horse, you will have a difficult time overcoming the negative association. Your goal for the moment is to teach the horse to walk in a circle around

Above: **Trotting on the longe line. Be sure not to wrap the longe line around your wrist. If the horse pulls, it is easy to get hurt.**

you, responding to voice commands to walk and halt.

Begin by positioning the foal broadside. Hold the longe line in your left hand, making sure that any extra length is carefully coiled to avoid tripping over it. Place the whip in your right hand and face the side of the foal. Slowly walk backwards away from the foal to the center of the circle.

The hardest part will be trying to make your horse understand what it is you want him to do. He has never walked in a circle on command before so the idea is completely alien to him. For this reason, many trainers like to have an assistant. While you are stationed in the center of the circle, your assistant stands near the horse, ready to show the horse what to do. Begin by giving the verbal command to walk. Your assistant will start the horse moving by leading him by the halter. When the horse begins to walk steadily, the assistant should release the halter and walk alongside the horse. If all is proceeding smoothly, the assistant should drop back, allowing the horse to continue on his own. Finally, your assistant should step out of the picture and you should try to urge the horse on, using the whip if he hesitates. A light flick of the whip below the hocks should do the job, and some horses require only a little snap of the whip.

If you do not have the benefit of an assistant, limit yourself to only 10 feet of the line so that horse remains within easy reach of the

whip. As before, step back from the horse to your position in the ring. Command the horse to go forward and extend the whip horizontally, pointing it toward his hocks. He will probably need more encouragement, so flick the whip against his hocks or crack it. There's a good chance he'll start moving at a trot or even a canter rather than a walk. Don't be concerned about speed at this point; just be happy the horse is moving. If, on the other hand, the horse does not move, shorten the line and step within two or three feet of him. Extend your left arm outward as an encouragement to move in that direction. Move on the circle with the horse, using the whip to coax him along if needed. As he begins to walk steadily, you can begin to drop back to the center of the circle. If the horse stops or hesitates, step forward again to encourage him to continue.

If the horse steps out of the circle, go to him, taking up the slack in the line as you approach him. Do not pull him toward you because this will teach him to turn and face you in response to a tug on the longe line. If the horse turns to face you, bring him back into place immediately by yanking hard on the longe line and simultaneously pointing the whip at this shoulder to encourage him to stay on the circle. If he backs away from you, let him back into the fence and then move him back into place with the whip.

Once the horse has mastered moving in a circle—and this may take some time—you need to teach him to respond to your signals to alter

Above: **A woman uses the longe line to allow her horse to work off excess energy between events at a horse show.**

Above: **Your horse's training should include a lesson on how to stand. Horses need to learn to stand still for a variety of reasons, from grooming to judging for conformation.**

his speed or to stop. If he is cantering or trotting, give him the command to walk and try to encourage him to do so by snapping the longe line downwards several times. You can also try to slow him down by gently tugging on the longe line, providing you do not pull him off the track. If neither of these methods works, then bring him to a complete stop by telling him 'Whoa' as you walk sideways to intercept him. Your horse will soon learn that as you move toward him your aim is to stop him, and he will begin to slow down even before you reach him. This is a turning point in training because he has learned to do what you want—he is learning to obey you. Soon your voice alone or your voice assisted by a little snap downward on the longe line will bring him to a halt.

The next step is to teach the horse to move in the opposite direction. It is best to try to teach this during the first or second lesson so moving in only one direction does not become ingrained.

How much you accomplish in one lesson will depend on your horse. Walking in a circle is physically demanding on a horse. Stop when his body feels warm and is slightly moist with sweat.

VOICE COMMANDS. Your horse should already know the verbal commands for walk, whoa and trot, and over the next several days, you should review these verbal commands on the longe line. Once these commands are mastered, teach him to canter on command. If you like, you can teach him to reverse directions.

Some trainers like to vary their intonation on the commands 'Walk' and 'Trot' since both are short, one syllable words and could be confusing to the horse. 'Walk' is said gently, while 'trot' is given more emphasis.

In giving voice commands, speak only as loud as you need to be heard by the horse. There is no need to raise your voice. If the horse does not obey a command, shouting will serve no purpose. Instead, repeat the command again to make sure he has heard it and if he does not obey on the second command, then make him obey. As with training any sort of animal, from the beginning you must establish that you are in charge.

Bear in mind, however, that during the learning process the horse needs a little time to process the command. You will be able to tell if he appears to be 'thinking' about the command. If he is standing still, he will stiffen while he is processing the command, or if he is moving, his pace will falter. Once he relaxes or no longer hesitates, he has stopped concentrating on the command. Then, you must repeat it or take action to make him comply. In time, your horse will learn a voice command so well that he will obey immediately and no longer need time to think about it.

To reward your horse when he obeys, praise him and do not give him another command for a while. For example, if you have commanded him to walk, continue to walk around the circle a few more times, or if you have commanded him to stop, let him stand quietly for a few moments. Think of reward as a brief respite from the pressure that results from learning something new.

Don't try to teach your horse too many commands at once. He'll just become confused and frustrated, which will slow down the learning process. Give one command and allow your horse to go around the circle a few times before trying another command. That way he will know he is doing the right thing and feel reassured by the sameness of the action.

Teaching your horse to canter on the longe line will probably be more difficult than teaching him to walk or trot. Chances are he will become excited as you urge him into a canter and if he tries to pull away he will be harder to control than he is at a walk or a trot. When he is first learning to canter on command, do not be concerned about his leads and do not try to make him hold the canter for more than a few strides. Let him break into a trot, move around the circle a few times and then give him the command to canter again. Try to convey an attitude of encouragement or helpfulness rather than exasperation. He'll sense your mood and will become calmer.

When your horse is working well at all gaits, you can teach him to reverse directions at your command. Make sure the longe line is snapped under the halter. Bring him to a halt before ordering him to reverse. When he halts, switch hands for the line and the whip and give the command 'Reverse' or 'Change' while tugging on the line to encourage him to turn. Use the whip to block him if he attempts to move in the wrong direction and crack it, if necessary, to urge him in the right direction.

LINE-DRIVING. For driving, you will need two longe lines and a longeing cavesson or a halter. Some horses ignore a halter, but if your horse is well trained at longeing, a halter is fine. Do not yet use a driving bridle with a bit, as you run the risk of damaging the horse's mouth if he becomes excited during training. As with longeing, you should begin your lessons in an enclosed area. Controlling two lines is difficult to do at first and you can easily entangle your horse in them. If that should happen, drop the lines—which is one reason working in an enclosed area is such a good idea. Your horse won't be able to run very far if he should take it into his head to dash off. Watch yourself, too, so that you don't entangle yourself in the lines. Don't wrap the lines around your hand. If the horse pulls or takes off, you can break your hand or wrist. It is better to coil them neatly and hold them on your fingers.

If you are using a cavesson, fasten the lines to the side rings. If you are using a halter, attach the lines underneath. For the first lesson you will need to place the outside line around the horse's hindquarters. Be prepared for him to be startled by the pressure from the line when he moves.

As the horse is longed, the outside line should rest lightly above the hocks. With a little practice, you will learn just how much tension is needed to keep the line in place.

Begin with your horse at a walk, but don't be concerned if he goes faster. The second line is unnerving to him so he needs a little time to become accustomed to it. When he realizes that the line will not hurt him he will calm down and you can take control of his pace. Put him at a walk and take a few steps toward his hindquarters and start walking in a small circle inside the larger circle he is walking in. At this point you are half longeing, half driving him, which will be somewhat puzzling to your horse. His pace may falter, in which case you should flip the outside driving line against his hindquarters to

Above: Leading the horse at a walk. The man in the foreground of the photo is examining the horse's way of going and conformation in preparation for shoeing the horse.

Above: **Before you ever put a saddle on your horse, his training will be quite extensive. He will have learned to wear a halter and to move at your command. Most of all, he will have learned to trust you.**

encourage him to go on. When he is moving steadily, increase the size of the circle, gradually dropping back until the horse is ahead of you. Stay to his left rather than directly behind him so that you can easily step back into the longe circle if you need to control him.

Eventually your ever-increasing circle will reach the limits of the enclosed area. When that happens, drive him around to the left of the enclosure and begin working back into a longeing circle and switch back to longing instead of driving. Stop the horse, let him take a brief break and then repeat the process going in the other direction. Then end the lesson for the day.

In the second lesson, you can teach your horse to turn and halt in response to commands from the lines. To teach him to turn, drive him through figure eights and each time you change directions, cross over behind him and guide him into the new direction. During the early lessons, make all the turns easy and gradual.

When he seems to be learning how to turn, begin teaching him how to halt. Step into position directly behind him, slow down and simply stop. Don't pull on the line; just let him feel like he has encountered a barrier—that he has gone as far as he can. Because this is the same technique that you used to teach him how to stop him while being led on a halter, he should readily understand what is required of him. Always reinforce hand aids with verbal aids.

If your horse is making progress with turns and halting, you can take him out of the enclosure for your third lesson. Turning him between bushes and trees will help you fine tune his response to your turning signals, and with a larger area to work in, you can

lighten the pressure on your horse by making fewer stops and starts.

Line-driving is especially useful in training at this point for two reasons. First, it reinforces the discipline of work. The better your horse responds to your commands to walk, trot and so on, the better prepared he will be to follow your orders when you ride him. Second, line-driving allows you to give your horse cross-country experience. As the two of you explore new territories, the bond between you will grow stronger. As your horse encounters new obstacles—such as a fallen log that you drive him over—he will learn to obey and more importantly to trust you completely.

TRAILER TRAINING

Your horse's early training should include trailer training. All too often people don't bother to introduce their horses to entering a trailer until it becomes necessary for the horse to be transported. Because the experience is alien to him, he balks, the owner forces him in and loading the horse into a trailer is a problem thereafter. Of course, this is a worst case scenario. Some trainers never have a problem on the first try, but to avoid a possible problem it's best to include trailer training as part of your horse's early schooling.

Horses are fearful of anything that feels insubstantial so be sure

Above: **Line-driving is the first step in training a horse to wear a harness.**

Above: Show horses especially must be trailer trained. Here, a horse backs out of a trailer. It is also important for a horse to accept standing in his trailer. On these occasions, make sure the windows are open so that he has plenty of fresh air.

that the trailer is hitched securely and will not tip forward or backward. If possible use a two-horse model so that you can lead him in from the other side of the partition if necessary. Before beginning the lesson, open the doors wide, and if there are windows, open them to give the trailer a light and airy atmosphere. Plan the lesson for a time when you know your horse will be a little hungry and have some grain placed in the tray inside the trailer to act as both inducement and reward.

Using an extra long lead line, about 10 to 12 feet long, lead your horse to the entry door of the trailer. If the horse becomes nervous and turns sideways as you reach the entry, just stop as if that had been your plan all along. When he relaxes, step into the trailer, leaving your horse at the doorway (on the long lead line). Walk toward the front of the trailer and rustle the grain so he knows it is there. Next, step out of the trailer and exchange the long lead for a short one.

Position yourself by your horse's left shoulder and lead him away from the trailer and then immediately approach the door again. Your objective is to see if your horse will enter the trailer voluntarily. As you near the door, lead the horse by the halter, reassuring him as you go. If you are extremely lucky, he will go right in.

If the horse doesn't enter the trailer, replace the short lead with the long one. Once again, go inside of the trailer. Your horse will no doubt prefer to stay outside. Encourage him to come in by gently moving the line–do not tug on it–and rustling the grain. His reluctance stems from his fear, not from contrariness; therefore, you need patience in order to assure him there is nothing to be afraid of. Keep encouraging him to enter the trailer. Don't allow him to simply stand around admiring the scenery. He'll probably make a few false starts just to check out the situation before he finally does enter the trailer. Don't shut the door immediately. Let the horse get used to walking in and out first. If the door is shut too quickly, the horse may panic at being enclosed and can learn to fear the trailer. The entire process may have taken a good 15 minutes, but it was 15 minutes well spent. Your horse now understands there is nothing to fear. The next lesson will take much less time and within a week your horse will enter a trailer without so much as a moment's hesitation.

After the first few lessons, stop using the long lines. As soon as possible encourage your horse to walk into the trailer unassisted. A well-trained horse will enter a trailer on his own, while his trainer waits outside to close the door.

UNLOADING THE HORSE. After your horse has entered the trailer for the first time, tie his halter rope with a slip knot so he cannot twist sideways and allow him to eat the grain. Since entering a trailer is only a portion of what your horse needs to understand about trailers, it's a good idea to take him for a short ride to acquaint him with the sensation of riding in a trailer. Make the ride as smooth as possible so that the experience is a positive one. Accelerate and reduce speeds gradually and take turns slowly. Too much jostling will make the horse feel jittery and could result in a horse that hates to travel. As a final precaution, drive slowly on dusty roads. Horses have been known to suffocate from dust blowing in off the roads.

When you stop to unload the horse, make him stand in the trailer for a short while. On numerous occasions, your horse will have to wait in a trailer, so it is important that he doesn't expect to be let out as soon as the trailer stops. Open the windows and one of the trailer doors, leaving the guard chain fastened, to make sure he has enough air.

The first step in unloading the horse is to untie the halter rope. This step is crucial because if the horse tries to back up while the rope is tied, he could end up with only his hind feet on the ground, which could spook him.

After untying the halter rope, quietly open the trailer door and let down the guard chain. Step in the trailer beside the horse and give him a reassuring pat. Wait a moment or two and then grasp the halter and tell him 'Back.' Very likely he will feel anxious, so take it slow and easy. If he hurries, he could easily bump his head or lose his footing.

PRELIMINARY SADDLE TRAINING

I n the days of the Wild West, the way to saddle train a horse was simply to throw a saddle on his back and then jump on and let the horse buck until he was completely exhausted. Sometimes the method worked, but the horses were often mean. Today, trainers are wiser. They realize that the best approach to training horses is to allay their instinctive fears and to win their confidence and respect.

Trainers may vary in their basic techniques, with some concentrating only on ground manners, while others favor longeing over line driving, or vice versa. Most agree, however, that a horse should not be saddle trained until he is three years old. Even though some two-year-olds are ridden, at that age they are not yet physically mature and permanent damage to bones, tendons and ligaments can result.

If you are a novice trainer, your horse will benefit from thorough training in longeing and line-driving. You would also be wise to seek assistance from an experienced trainer who knows how bad habits *start* and can help you avoid them.

SADDLING YOUR HORSE FOR THE FIRST TIME. Before you mount your horse for the first time, introduce him to the equipment you will be using. The type of saddle that you use for training–be it a stock saddle or a flat saddle–is unimportant. What does matter is that the saddle is comfortable for both you and the horse.

Everything you have done up to this point has been in preparation for the first moment you sit in the saddle. In addition to longeing and line-driving, there are several other little things you can do to help you prepare your horse for the saddle. For example, while grooming

Above: A frequent participant at horse shows and exhibitions, this Clydesdale calmly allows his trainer to lead him from the trailer.

Above: Sarah Cohen with Azul. This all-purpose saddle can be used for both dressage and jumping.

your horse you can lean over him to accustom him to weight on his back, or you can stand on a fence rail next to him so that you are taller than he is—as you will be when you are on his back.

Poor saddle training now can result in problems that can persist for a lifetime. Some horses become so saddle-shy that they always cringe when a saddle is lifted toward them. Some horses, though not afraid of a saddle, are permitted to fidget while being saddled; others learn to puff up whenever the girths are tightened. Perhaps the worst problem of all is cinch-bound horses—horses that sink or throw themselves to the ground when the girth is drawn tight. These problems illustrate why it is so important to have an experienced trainer to assist you in training your young horse. With a little care and forethought, your horse need never develop any problems about being saddled.

An effective method for preparing your horse for the feeling of a girth is to longe him with a surcingle. Put the surcingle on him, tighten it just enough to hold it in place, longe him and then tighten the surcingle a bit more and longe him again. When tightening the surcingle or any type of girth make sure your actions are smooth and swift. Clumsy saddling on your part can produce a problem horse. You also need to watch for drawing a girth too suddenly or severely—this is what causes cinch-bound horses.

After your horse has been longed with the surcingle, remove it and introduce him to the saddle pad. Show him the pad, rub it against him and then place it on his back. His early training should have prepared him for this type of handling, but if he is at all anxious, don't push him. Let him become accustomed to the pad at his own pace. Once he has calmed down, leave the pad on for a few moments, take it off and repeat the process several times.

If possible have an assistant hold your horse the first time you place the saddle on the horse's back. That way, you can have a firm hold on the saddle and prevent it from slipping if the horse is startled. A saddle that slips and falls off a horse can easily frighten a horse, making him saddle-shy.

As you place the saddle on his back, be sure that your mood is confident and reassuring. If you are too rough you will frighten him, while a too timid approach may make him uneasy. After you have placed the saddle on his back, leave it there for just a few moments, keeping your hands on it to steady it. Jostle the saddle slightly so that your horse will understand that it is harmless. Take the saddle off and repeat the process several times. Your goal is to make your horse feel comfortable about this strange new process. Remember, he fears what he does not understand.

When your horse seems comfortable with the saddle, leave it on

Above: A Western saddle. Regardless of the type of saddle used, it's important to teach your horse proper saddle manners right from the start. Don't allow him to fidget when you place the saddle on his back, or to puff himself up when the girth is tightened.

Above: **The first time you mount your horse, put your left foot in the stirrup and lightly bounce up and down in the stirrup a few times until the horse is accustomed to your weight.**

and tighten the girth. If you trained him with the surcingle and the longe line, he should not object. Draw the girth tight enough to hold the saddle in place but not as tight as you would need for riding.

As mentioned earlier, you must be quick when you tighten the girth. Even though you have prepared your horse for this moment, he may still feel startled when he realizes the saddle is being pinned to his back. If you don't act quickly, the saddle may slip underneath him, which may make him kick and struggle.

When the girth is secure, lead your horse on a longe line. If the horse objects to the saddle and starts to buck, a longe line will give you more control than a shorter lead. If he starts to struggle, give him room and let him discover that he cannot get rid of the saddle. When he settles down, continue to lead him. Do not allow him to stop and graze, or he may forget that he is saddled and will be upset when he rediscovers that he is.

To conclude the lesson, longe him with the saddle. Once again he may buck, but continue the lesson as soon as he quiets down. Spend the next few days, longeing him with the saddle.

SELECTING A BIT AND BRIDLE. A bit is designed to give the trainer control over his horse. Control is achieved, to a greater or lesser degree, through pain. During the early stages of training, all a trainer needs to be concerned with is a means for turning, slowing and halting the horse. At this stage of training the specific type of bit— snaffle, curb and so on—is secondary. What matters is that you can control your horse without making him frightened or defiant. Later on when you are training your horse for a certain specialty, the specific type of bit needed takes on more importance.

Problems with bits result because a bit is misused. For a novice, the best way to select a bit is to rely on the advice of an experienced trainer.

Introducing your horse to a bit is a gradual process. Begin by having the horse wear a bridle with a snaffle for about an hour every day for several days. He can wear the snaffle in his stall and while being longed, but do not attach any reins to the snaffle. Leading or longeing should be done by a halter only. The bit in his mouth will understandably be confusing to the horse. He will shake his head, chew on the bit and try to work it out of his mouth, but within a few days, he will be used to it.

When he is used to the feeling of the bit in his mouth, line-drive him with the snaffle. (Do not use a curb bit for this, as a curb bit used under these circumstances can cause your horse to overflex his neck.) Your horse should accept the snaffle fairly readily if he has been thoroughly introduced to line driving with a halter. Do all your work at a walk and all turns and halts should be gentle. Ultimately, you want your horse to stop on just a light signal. To teach him to respond to your signal, use a voice command to halt *before* you use the lines, and never pull forcefully on the lines. As you did in your earlier training, let the horse sense resistance.

The first time you use the bit to stop the horse, he will probably be confused and will not understand that you want him to stop. Do not turn the lesson into a struggle. Relax the lines, let him move forward a few steps and then repeat the voice command and the signal. As you have seen before, once your horse discovers he has nothing to fear, he will do what you ask.

This time is a learning period for the novice trainer as well as the horse, for the novice is learning how to use his hands–how to control a horse. If you notice that your horse opens his mouth wide before he comes to a complete stop, then you are not giving your horse enough time to stop. Instead, you are unconsciously pulling him to a stop. The horse should learn to respond to the lines without opening his mouth and bowing his head.

Later on, your horse may refuse to reduce his pace when you give him the signal on the lines. If he shows no sign of fear, he is testing you. If this happens, stand firm and do not give into your horse. He will pull hard, but this is a test of wills. It is natural for a horse to make one last try before yielding to a new kind of control.

To teach your horse to turn with a bit, use the same technique of resisting rather than pulling that you used when teaching him to halt. You will know you are pulling too hard if your horse 'rubber-necks' (overbends his neck sideways before and during a turn).

Putting a bridle on a horse correctly is just as important as proper saddle handling. Horses that object to bridling by jerking their heads or refusing to open their mouths for the bit were handled poorly during training and may even have been punished for their misbehavior.

Putting a bridle on a young horse for the first time requires patience and gentle handling even though he is used to wearing a halter. The bit, of course, is the tricky part. To get a horse to open his mouth for a bit, insert your thumb in the corner of his mouth and press downward on the bar of the jaw. As soon as his mouth opens, slip the bit into place and quickly but smoothly adjust the headstall. If you are slow about placing the crownpiece over the ears, the bit is allowed to dangle loosely, making the horse nervous. In time your horse will learn to open his mouth on his own and take the bit. Encourage him to do this by holding the bit *gently* against his teeth for a few seconds before you open his mouth with your thumb.

Taking off the bridle requires as much care as putting it on does. Slip the crownpiece over the ears and allow the horse to relax his mouth and work the bit forward. Otherwise, the bit will bang against his teeth, and can make him resist bridling.

FIRST MOUNTING. The care that has guided you through your horse's preliminary training should be no less on this important day. Even the weather should be a consideration: a windy day will distract a horse, while cold weather is stimulating.

Begin by saddling and bridling your horse and then give him a workout on the longe line to calm him down. Have an assistant hold the horse by a lead or longe line while you mount him. The assistant's task is to keep the horse steady; there is no need to grip the horse tightly.

Your horse is unaccustomed to carrying weight so you must introduce this concept to him gradually. Put your hand in the left stirrup and if the horse reacts well, try it again, this time using your foot. Remove your foot and pause briefly before trying it a few more times. With only your foot in the stirrup, bounce up and down

Above: With your left foot in the stirrup, swing your right leg over the horse, keeping your weight as evenly distributed as possible. Note that the trainer has balanced his weight by placing his right hand on the saddle.

Above: **Children can be effective trainers because they easily develop a rapport with the horse.**

lightly to give the horse some feeling of weight.

When your horse seems unconcerned about your bouncing in the stirrup, go one step further and lean across the saddle for about a minute. Remove your weight *before* he has the chance to get upset. However, if he appears upset, go back to bouncing in the saddle. End the lesson after he has accepted some part of the lesson. You don't want to teach him that he can get out of being mounted by getting upset. If your horse accepted this last step relatively calmly, then mount him astride. Keep your body bent low, straightening up gradually. No matter how placid he has been up to this point, he will be startled to have you towering above him. Sit quietly in the saddle for a moment and then dismount.

The next few days should be spent practicing mounting and dismounting. It's a good practice to longe him first to work off any excess energy. Each time stay in the saddle a bit longer, eventually working up to several minutes. When your horse calmly accepts mounting and dismounting, alter your careful approach. Brush his ears or rub against his side to acquaint him with the unexpected.

RIDING YOUR HORSE

Above: Once your horse has learned to accept the saddle, you are ready to ride him. The first few sessions should be limited to walking in an enclosed area.

After a few days of practice mounting and dismounting, you and your horse are ready for your first ride. Even though he is used to the feeling of someone on his back, he is not used to carrying someone. Moreover, each of the gaits will feel differently to him, so you need to give him time to adjust to walking before you progress to trotting and so on. During the early stages of riding, restrict your lessons to a small enclosure and then a large arena before you attempt trail riding. Riding in an enclosed area gives you better control over your horse.

The goal in riding is to get the horse to respond to the way you shift your weight and to your leg signals. Use the least amount of hand pressure as possible.

To make the horse move forward, squeeze both legs. Of course,

Above: Backing. To teach your horse to move backwards, put your weight in your heels. Squeeze with your thighs while having firm contact with the horse's mouth. The horse needs to learn to move backwards away from the tension on his mouth. Use light, equal pressure from both your calves to encourage him to back in a straight line.

this signal is completely alien to your horse so there's a good chance he'll just stand there. If so, have a friend lead the horse for you. Try this several times, each time using the leg signal before your helper leads the horse. Your horse will soon understand the leg signal means go forward.

For English riding, hold the reins in two hands, keeping them slack except when signaling to turn or halt. Do not pull on the reins to stop the horse. Use the verbal command to halt in conjunction with hand and leg signals. Let your hands *signal* a stop, as in line-driving. If your horse does not yield to the tension on the reins, keep one hand firmly in place and tug back quickly with the other. The one-rein motion will break up the horse's resistance. Repeat your original signal to halt. He should be ready to obey, both mentally and physically. Mentally, you have gotten his attention, and physically, his balance has shifted rearward in preparation for stopping.

The goal with turning is to make the horse turn in response to your leg signals while you use the reins as you did in line driving. You will need to give him as much help as possible, making the turns wide and gradual. You may also need to lead him through the turn by extending your active hand, taking care not to restrain him accidentally with your other hand.

Spend about a week practicing walking. You may find it helpful to have a friend ride along on an older, experienced horse. Your horse will gain a level of confidence by following the other horse.

Even though your riding sessions are going well, the experience is still novel for your horse and he may be easily startled or simply try to rebel. If this happens, there are several guidelines you need to bear in mind. Do not pull on the reins or squeeze tighter with your legs. Your horse will only struggle more. Instead, concentrate on staying relaxed and supple so that you can move *with* the horse. Do not try to calm your horse down by patting him or talking to him reassuringly. He might interpret your actions as positive reinforcement for his behavior. Do not dismount—this is what the horse wants. Obviously, there are times when dismounting is the only safe course of action. In those cases, remount as quickly as you can.

During the early stages of training, a riding crop is an effective tool for teaching your horse to go forward. It is *not* used for punishment. Rather, the crop is used to reinforce the rider's leg signals. If your horse does not respond to your leg signals, you can tap him with the crop, encouraging him to go forward. The first time you use the crop, reach behind you and tap him behind your leg. The pressure from behind should be enough inducement to urge him forward. If the horse is startled by the crop and does not respond, tap him again. He will soon associate the tap with the request to move forward. Some trainers recommend the use of spurs over a riding crop. *Beginners should not use spurs.* The drawback to spurs is that no matter how blunt they are, their pricking often causes the horse to become a tail switcher. Tail switching is a reflexive action caused by the horse's desire to remove an annoyance. Tail switching can easily become a nervous habit and be very difficult to break. When used by an experienced horsemen on a well-trained horse, spurs can be useful. In training, however, a riding crop is the better choice.

THE TROT. Once your horse is comfortable at a walk you can begin schooling in the trot. If possible, you should continue conducting the lessons in an arena. When you decide it is time to introduce the trot, squeeze with your calves to tell him to trot. Use verbal commands in conjunction with the leg signal to help him understand what you want. He may only trot a few steps before going back to a walk. This is to be expected and is an indication that the horse is *not* anxious. Let him walk a while and then urge him to trot again, just as you did before. Remember that even though he knows how to trot, the sensation of trotting while carrying someone is a new sensation. As you have noticed throughout the training of your horse, he needs time to adjust to new situations, so keep your first trotting lesson short.

In the next lesson, work on having the horse maintain the trot for longer periods. Sometimes a horse will 'hump up' while trotting because of the strange sensation on his back. If this happens, ignore the behavior as much as possible. Keep the reins light and urge him forward. Stopping will give him the opportunity to buck.

During the early stages of training, your goal is to teach the horse to maintain a steady pace. You need to find a rate of speed that is natural and comfortable for the horse. His tendency will be to move too fast and break into a canter. If you notice his breathing quicken and his stride becoming uneven, he is reaching the breaking point of his gait. When you see this happening, reduce his pace to keep him at a trot.

At this stage in training, your horse's trot will be rough because he is moving fairly fast. To make the ride easier on both you and the horse, you can post at the trot, if you ride English. When posting at the trot, the rider moves up and down in the saddle in rhythm with the movement of the horse. In a trot, the left foreleg and the right hind leg move forward as one diagonal pair, and the right foreleg and the left hind leg move as the other. To post on the outside diagonal, the rider rises when the horse's outside foreleg is reaching forward. Hunter and saddle horse classes in horse shows in the United States require that a rider post on the outside diagonal along the rail and through turns; however, it is better for the horse if a rider learns to vary the diagonals while riding cross-country. That way, the horse will avoid becoming one-sided and the muscles will be evenly worked.

One way to teach your horse to steady his trot is to practice 'schooling figures,' such as circles, half-circles and figure eights. The figures should be ridden accurately and conscientiously. Always make the circle completely round and always begin them at the same point. To ride a circle, leave the track along the side of the arena and return to the same point from which you departed. The circle should be no less than six meters (20 feet) in diameter. For a half-circle, leave the track as you would for a full circle. At the halfway point, return on a diagonal line to the starting point. Half-circles can also be ridden in reverse by leaving the track on a diagonal line to a point about six or nine meters (20 or 30 feet) from the track and then returning to the track in a half-circle. Begin a figure eight at the point where the two circles meet. Make sure that the two circles are perfectly formed.

Schooling figures are useful in training because they help a horse

Above: **The canter. This is a fast gait of three beats that always leads off from one of the hind legs. There is a moment of suspsension when all four feet are in the air. Then, the front legs strike the ground in a rolling motion and the horse' weight rests again on the hindquarters. This action, reapeated over and over, causes the undulating movement of the canter.**

Above: **Wearing a hunt cap is a good safety precaution whenever riding a horse. Some horses can be easily startled and can throw even an experienced rider, or a horse may miss a jump and send the rider tumbling.**

Facing page: **Two young riders prepare for a pleasant ride through the English countryside.**

improve his balance and suppleness with a rider on his back. In addition, simply walking or trotting around an arena can grow boring for a young horse, so most horses will benefit from the change of pace provided by the figures.

During this stage of your horse's training, you should plan on spending about an hour a day in the arena working with your horse. However, the entire hour is not devoted to non-stop work. At first, work for no more than 20 minutes, giving your horse frequent rest periods in which you allow the horse to stand quietly or walk on a loose rein. These rest periods are learning sessions in their own right. Allowing your horse to stand still while you are on his back teaches him a skill that you will value later. If all you do is ride the horse while you are mounted on him, that is what he will expect to do and chances are that he will grow fidgety if asked to stand.

THE CANTER. The time required between introducing the trot and introducing the canter will depend on the individual horse. Most people wait several months before teaching the canter. It takes hours of trotting and doing schooling figures for the horse to learn

Above: A trainer uses a longe line to exercise her horse after riding in a trailer. After a long ride, the horse will be bursting with pent up energy and eager to run. Be sure to let him work up to a gallop gradually so that he doesn't strain any muscles.

to balance well at the trot. A horse should not be taught to canter until he is well balanced at the trot.

The large arena is the best place to introduce the canter because there is enough room for the horse to maintain his pace while giving the rider enough control. Wait until the end of the session to introduce the canter so that the horse has had ample opportunity to work off excess energy. Whereas the signal for the trot is squeezing with both legs, the signal for the canter is the outside leg behind the girth and the inside leg on the girth. Use a verbal command to reinforce the leg signal. As before, he will drop into the new stride briefly before falling back into the old one. When he falls back into the trot, let him maintain it until he is comfortable and urge him into the canter again. Regardless of how long he holds the canter, let him know he has done well by ending the lesson.

Though unlikely, there are a couple of scenarios for which you should be prepared when you introduce the canter. Your horse may be startled when introduced and may react by bucking slightly. If he does, leave the reins light and urge him forward. Another possibility is that he may pick up speed instead of dropping back into a trot. Under these circumstances he probably will not respond to your signal to halt and rather than trying to force him to stop, which will only make matters worse, work on *guiding* him. Guide him into a large circle and keep him on the circle until he tires. Then, after a walk to cool and calm him, try the canter again.

At first, the canter will be rough and fast. He will tend to fall into a trot when he slows his pace or he will go too fast and break into a gallop. Your goal for now is to stabilize the canter on a light rein. Later on you can teach him specific signals for leads. However, you should work on varying leads so he doesn't start to favor a side.

When your horse has learned to respond to your signals to walk, trot, canter and halt, you can devote your lessons to polishing these skills. For both you and your horse, the best and most enjoyable way to practice is trail riding. During this time, you are concentrating only on those skills you have already worked on with your horse. You and your horse are exploring new territories and getting better acquainted, and the more time you can spend trail riding, the better. When you return to the arena, you can work on whatever type of advanced schooling you want to pursue.

Make your first few excursions from the stable as uneventful as possible. Avoid anything that could excite your horse–traffic, steep inclines, deep streams or creeks, creaky bridges, swampy ground. Plan a route that covers a smooth, easy terrain, and spend most of the time at a walk.

The presence of a quiet, older horse or other horses can have a positive influence on your horse. When you encounter an obstacle, such as a creek, your horse will be more willing to cross the creek if he can follow the older horse. When introducing your horse to traffic, have another rider positioned between your horse and the road. If the traffic does not seem to bother your horse, you can soon drop back behind the other horse. Once your horse is accustomed to his trail rides at a walk, you can try the trot, using the terrain to your advantage. If you start him moving on a slight incline, he will be forced to steady his pace. Make sure the incline is a *slight* one, and don't allow him to trot downhill, as this can put too much pressure on his forelegs. Cantering can be introduced in the same manner. Once again, make sure that the inclines are slight.

If you have been riding with friends and your horse is making good progress, start riding on your own, as your horse must learn to be independent. Horses are, by nature, herd bound. One way to wean him from the other horses is to take brief excursions on your own while you are out riding with other people. When you finally do take him out on his own, you'll notice that your horse is much more easily frightened by objects along the way. Even something as innocuous as a leaf blowing across the trail can spook a horse. Talking calmly while you urge him on is a useful way of reassuring your horse when you are asking him to do something new or scarey. Stopping to reassure him can have just as harmful an effect as pulling sharply on the reins. You may find yourself in a situation in which your horse is so frightened, he refuses to go past the object that has terrified him. In that case, dismount and gradually lead your horse to the object, taking it a step at a time so that he can evaluate the situation.

THE GALLOP. You can introduce your horse to a gallop on one of your trail rides, providing you choose a smooth terrain free of ditches and holes. A slight hill works well as horses are sometimes hard to stop and going up hill tires them. Be sure to avoid galloping on a downhill slope where your horse could easily stumble and fall. You can also try galloping in a large arena, which will give you room to circle if your horse doesn't want to stop.

Start by putting your horse into a trot, then a canter, finally easing him into a controlled gallop. Speed excites a horse, but if you move into a gallop smoothly and easily your horse should not be frightened. After several galloping sessions spread out over a period of days, you can ease him into a full gallop. The point here is to show him there is nothing to fear. Because he is still a young horse, you don't want to overdo galloping. He has not yet learned to balance himself as he runs.

BACKING. It is not difficult to teach your horse to back up, but the lesson should wait until he has been conditioned to go forward willingly. As you have learned previously, it is crucial that you do not pull. Apply a small amount of pressure to the bit and hold it. The horse will feel uncomfortable and will try to ease his discomfort. He may, for example, tug against your hands, or he may dip his nose toward his chest. If he tugs, resist the tugging, keeping your hands firm. If he dips his nose, lift up on one rein to raise his head and then re-apply the pressure. Eventually, the horse will move back—which is exactly what you want. As soon as he steps back, reward him by releasing the pressure. Then step forward so that he will learn from the start that stepping backwards will be followed by stepping forward. For the first few lessons, work on only one or two steps back. As his confidence develops, ask him for more. At this point, your horse's 'basic training' is complete. You have the option of pursuing a number of different specialty areas, with competition as your goal; however, you need not school your horse for competition. Your horse is now a well-trained mount and a joy to ride.

Above: The halt. Your goal is to teach the horse to stop voluntarily in response to your aids–pressure from your legs and on the reins. Notice the trainer has a firm grip on the reins, but is not tugging on them. The horse must stand straight with his feet forming a square.

A BRIEF GUIDE TO GROOMING YOUR HORSE

All horses, whether prize show horses or companions, need proper care and grooming. Coats need to clipped, and for show purposes, manes may need to be pulled and tails braided. Horses, of course, must be bathed and sprayed with fly repellents, and their hooves conditioneed and polished.

Bathing your horse with a hose is a fairly simple procedure. With the water at low pressure, begin by spraying first his legs, shoulders, back, sides and hips. Give him time to adjust to the cold temperature of the water before you increase the water pressure. Horses hate water in their ears so be sure to keep the hose away from your horse's head. Use a sponge instead of the hose.

Because many grooming aids are available as sprays, your horse must learn to accept the hissing sound of the spray container. As you

Above: **Applying fly spray. Horses must be introduced to the hissing sound of a spray container so that they will stand patiently while you spray them.** *Facing page:* **Grooming is an on-going process, but a brief grooming session at the horse show will make both horse and rider feel better. Here, a handler and her freshly groomed horse leave the horse barns and head for the ring.**

Below: **A trainer bathes his horse while an assistant holds the lead.**

Shoeing the horse. *Counterclockwise, from the right:* 1) A farrier examines the hoof and shoes to determine wear or stress points. 2) Using pulloffs, the farrier starts at the heels and lifts the old shoe away from the hoof with a motion toward the center of the hoof. 3) He then uses nippers to clip the hoof wall, keeping the nippers at a perpendicular angle to the hoof.

have discovered with other aspects of training, the best approach is a gradual one. Introduce your horse to the sprayer by letting him see and hear it *before* you aim it at him. Use an all-purpose sprayer filled with water and spray the air around him a few times–more if he seems ill at ease. Some horses will not be nervous at all but others will require more time to adjust to the sprayer. Begin by spraying only his forefeet. The next day spray his legs too. Spray him more each day until you can spray his entire body. By this time, you should understand your horse well and will know how quickly he accepts something new. During fly season, fly spray is essential, so your horse must be trained to stand patiently while you spray his body, neck and legs, and apply a special repellant to his face. If you have not taken the time to introduce your horse to this process, you run the risk of being kicked.

In addition to these basic aspects of grooming, there are few areas of horse care that are more important than the care of the hoof. Hooves must be cleaned regularly, and if the horse is stabled, the stall must be kept clean and dry to prevent disease. Care of the hoof begins when a foal is very young. Foals will naturally get plenty of exercise, and in most cases, they are not subjected to long hours on a hard street, or miles over rocky terrain, which can damage the hoof. On the other hand, if they are reared around a barn, or in a small lot, their hooves do not receive sufficient wear and various unhealthy conditions can develop. For example, if the wall of the hoof becomes too long, it often separates from the sole, bending slightly and can lead to lameness if left unchecked.

The owner should leave shoeing and trimming to a farrier, but the owner needs to check the hooves daily and know how to recognize the signs of common hoof problems. The hoof grows about an inch

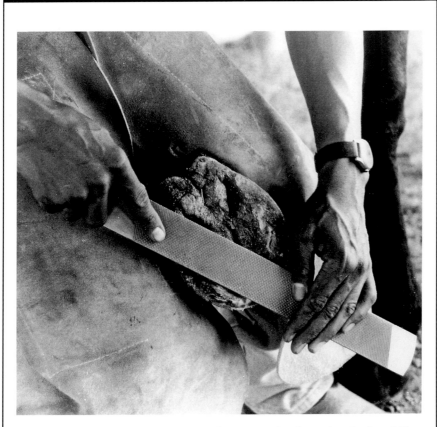

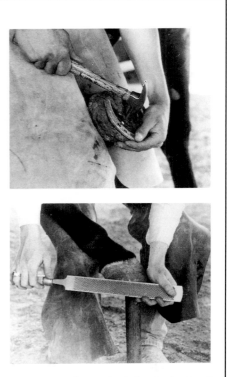

Clockwise, from the left: **1) The hoof wall is rasped, or filed, to the proper depth and balance. 2) The farrier nails the shoe to the hoof. 3) The farrier cleans under the clinch.**

during a three-month period, so the general rule is that it should be trimmed midway through that period. The unshod hoof grows faster than it wears off unless the horse is in very rocky terrain. There, it can wear faster than it grows and the horse can become 'sore-footed.'

If the horse is shod, shoes should be reset about every five or six weeks. Many horses tend to 'run' (wear) their shoes more on one side than the other just as people will wear their shoe heels more on one side. The way a hoof wears is also affected by the legs. Some horses are 'cow-hocked' (the hocks, or hind knees, tend to curve in toward each other) behind, while many are 'knock-kneed' or 'bandy-legged' (ill-shaped front legs) in front. The owner should check the hooves daily to make sure the shoes are not loose and examine the hooves for cracks and to make sure they are neither too dry nor too wet. If there is a problem with dryness or wetness, a variety of products are available for conditioning.

Thrush is one of the most common problems affecting the hooves, but it is one that can be easily detected–by sight and smell. Thrush makes the horn of the frog (the horny formation lying like a wedge between the two turned-in bars of the hoof) ragged and bad smelling, and a dark liquid collects in the cleft. As time goes on, the frog band will be affected, and irregular rings and cross rings will form on the wall. The cause is usually lack of exercise in fresh air, or the frog being pared too closely. Other causes may also include prolonged standing in a dirty, wet stall or lot, or the use of frog pads for several months. If detected early, thrush can be treated by applying the appropriate solution. Advanced cases should be handled by a farrier or a veterinarian, who will trim the frog.

SHOWING YOUR HORSE

Horse shows run the gamut from conformation judging *(above)* to horse pulling *(below)*, an event that tests the brute strength of the horse. Events of this sort are typically held at state and county fairs across the United States.

Facing page: **Part of the show scene is simply waiting for your event to begin.**

The first competitive horse shows probably took place as early as the eighth century BC, and existed in some way ever since. The first shows tested the day-to-day skills of working horses; today, however, horse shows are devoted primarily to saddle and harness horses.

In the United States, most horse shows are organized by the American Horse Shows Association (AHSA). The shows are arranged in a number of different ways. Some are local shows lasting one day; others last for more than a week and include various types of performance at different levels. Typically, they run for two to three days, and may offer performance classes, in which the horse is judged on performance at various gaits or over fences; equitation classes, in which the rider is judged, and halter classes, in which the horse's physical conformation is judged. The AHSA establishes the rules and regulations for 23 different divisions, which run the gamut from Arabian to Western. The AHSA recognizes roughly 2500 shows each year. There are, of course, many informal events also held

Above: **Horse and rider compete in a Prix St Georges level dressage test at the San Francisco Equestrian Festival in June 1990. The Prix St Georges is the first level of international competition.**

throughout the country that are not sanctioned by the AHSA. These events can provide the novice with a good introduction to the show world.

The British Horse Society has even more divisions than the AHSA. The biggest event of the year is the Horse of the Year Show at Wembley Stadium. The show is open to all categories of horses that have distinguished themselves in their specific fields during the year. Dedicated to all types of horses, it is a thoroughly British celebration of an animal that has become an integral part of the culture. The show is a lively, spectacular event, opening with the Queen's Horse Guards. Then each horse parades through the stadium to much applause.

In addition to governing shows, the AHSA and the British Horse Society are responsible for recording show results; establishing, revising and enforcing regulations; registering members; and authorizing judges.

DRESSAGE

Dressage is both a method of training and a competitive sport. In short, dressage is the art of horse riding. The goal of dressage, as defined by the Fédération Equestre Internationale (FEI), the world governing body of horse sports, is 'the harmonious development of the physique and ability of the horse. As a result it makes the horse calm, supple, loose and flexible, but also confident, attentive and keen, thus achieving perfect understanding with his rider.'

These are qualities that all riders would want their horses to possess, and certainly all horses would benefit from what is loosely called 'basic dressage.' However, a distinction needs to be drawn between basic dressage as preparation for some other equestrian activity and dressage as a competitive discipline. At its highest levels—Olympic and World Cup—dressage is probably the most sophisticated and aesthetically pleasing of all equestrian events.

In dressage, the horse is controlled by 'aids'—a language between horse and rider that is communicated through the action of the reins, pressure of the legs or even a shift in the rider's weight. Neither voice commands nor a crop can be used. The horse must respond with complete obedience, smoothly carrying out whatever is required: turning left or right, lengthening or shortening the pace, two-track work and making smooth transitions from one pace to another.

As a result of dressage training, the horse becomes accustomed to controlling the use of his muscles, adopting the correct stance, balancing his weight, coordinating his movements and responding quickly and correctly to the slightest signal from the rider. Though physically demanding, the psychology of the individual horse clearly must come into play. Not all horses have the mental capabilities for dressage. Horses that are unstable, temperamental, too highly strung or uncooperative are inappropriate for dressage. The ideal dressage horse is healthy and intelligent with a natural tendency to obey. He must have a light, well-carried head, narrow ears, large eyes expressing keenness and concentration, powerful muscles, short loins, healthy legs and a good natural stance. The dressage horse is attractive, with a noble and graceful bearing.

Dressage horses can be of any breed, but historically horses of German breeding such as Hanoverian, Holsteiner, Trakehner and Rheinlander, the Swedish and Dutch warmbloods, and the French Selle Français have excelled at dressage, as they have been bred for that purpose for centuries. Thoroughbreds tend to be too high strung for dressage, but there have been notable exceptions.

The basic training for dressage is the same as for any other riding horse, except that the trainer may encourage the young horse to take the bit 'from behind,' so that the natural purity of the horse's gaits is preserved. Dressage emphasizes pushing the horse up to the bit through the rider's legs instead of controlling the horse primarily through the hands.

Much preliminary training is done with the horse loose or on a longe line because adjusting to the rider's weight is a considerable challenge for the young horse. For dismounted work 'in hand,' the horse is often harnessed with side reins attached to a girth or surcingle, which provides some support, much as a rider's hands would. When the horse has learned to accept a rider, the trainer's goal is to develop the horse's natural balance, rhythm, cadence, free forward movement and straightness. Training is ideally carried out in a special schooling area called a manège. Here, the horse is taught to execute the various geometric figures he will later perform in the arena. Beginning with simple circles, he will gradually progress to squares, serpentines, diagonals and various combinations thereof. The horse must be taught to form the figure precisely and accurately while maintaining his pace.

The horse must also learn 'transitions'—the instant change from one pace to another without any loss of control. Additionally, the horse will learn the proper way to carry his head and the various turns, including the demi-pirouette, the pirouette, the volte and the piaffes. Eventually, the horse will advance to collection. When a horse is collected his hocks are brought in beneath his body and flexed to lower the quarters. His pace is shortened and elevated and he is said to be collected 'between hand and leg.' Collection creates a great deal of muscle strain and should not even be attempted until the proper muscles have been developed. To put this into the proper perspective, consider that few horses reach the highest level of dressage competition before the age of eight. Sadly, many horses have been ruined by being asked to do advanced work before they were capable of it. For example, horses have been spoiled by having a double bridle (a requirement for the Grand Prix level) forced upon them before they have learned to accept the snaffle bridle that is required at the lower levels.

All of these movements are to be executed effortlessly, as if the horse were performing them of his own accord. The overall impression is one of grace and harmony, with horse and rider moving in perfect unison.

In competitive dressage, the horse and rider perform these move-

Above: **The working trot. This is a pace between the medium and collected trot in which the horse is properly balanced and goes forward with even, elastic steps.**

Above: In competitive dressage the horse and rider perform a prescribed test from memory. The spectator should be able to observe the differences between the paces. The transitions between the paces should be smooth, straight and definite. The rider's aids, however, should be invisible to the spectator.

ments in sequence in an arena measuring 20 by 60 meters (22 by 66 yards) in size. The ride must be done from memory, except at the lower levels of competition. The arena is marked by 12 lettered points (A K V E S H C M R B P F) around its circumference, with another five lettered points down the middle (D L X I G). Some tests are conducted in a smaller arena, which is 20 by 40 meters (22 by 44 yards). The origin of the letters is unknown and quite a puzzle, as there seems to be no logical basis behind them. The sequence of movements must be performed exactly where specified and within a given time.

The figures of dressage at all levels are scored according to the following scale:

10 Excellent	5 Sufficient
9 Very Good	4 Insufficient
8 Good	3 Fairly bad
7 Fairly Good	2 Bad
6 Satisfactory	1 Very Bad
0 Not executed	

Penalty points are incurred if the time is exceeded or if errors are committed in the sequence. If the horse and rider exceed the

allotted time, the presentation is not interrupted, but every second marked up incurs half a penalty point. Penalty points are also given if the contestant makes an 'error of the test' (trotting in the raised position rather than seated, does not take the reins in one hand at the salute, etc). When a contestant commits an 'error of the course' (takes a wrong turn, omits a movement), the chairman of the jury sounds a bell, unless it would affect the continuation of the presentation. Whether or not the bell is sounded, the error is penalized by two points the first time, by four points the second time, by eight points the third time, and by elimination the fourth time. The total number of penalty points is deducted from the marks awarded by the panel of judges for each movement and the transition between them.

If the horse or rider, or both, should fall, the contestant is penalized for the time lost as well as the effects the fall had on the execution of the movement. A contestant is also penalized for using voice or sounds. Contestants will be eliminated for entering the arena late or for using illegal equipment, such as special reins, rubber bits and cheekpieces, bandages or leg guards and blinkers.

Though the levels of competition in the United States and Britain are given different names, the requirements are roughly the same. (Note: The names of the British levels are listed parenthetically.)

At top: The extended trot. *Above:* A Lipizzaner of the world famous Spanish Riding School in Vienna.

Above: **The horse and rider's performance is evaluated by a panel of judges known as a jury. The judges will penalize for faults, but they must look for good as well as bad, and their comments must include praise as well as criticism.**

The objective of the Training Level (Preliminary) is to introduce the horse and rider to the basic principles of competition. Horses must carry out the basic paces, the free walk, and ride circles of 20 meters (22 yards) in diameter. Progressive transitions are permitted. For example, the horse may walk a few steps as he moves from trot to halt. Judges are looking for 'obedience' to the aids of the rider; for free, rhythmic, forward movement; and for stretching into the bit in a calm, receptive manner.

In the First Level (Novice), the objective is to determine that the correct foundation is being laid for successful training of the horse. The horse should move freely forward in a relaxed, rhythmic manner and accept the bit and obey the aids of the rider. Horses are required to perform serpentines at the trot, show lengthened strides at the trot, lengthened strides at the canter (US only) and perform 10-meter (11 yards) circles (15 meters (16.5 yards) in Great Britain) at the trot. Transitions should be less progressive.

By the time a horse has reached the Second Level (Elementary and Advanced Elementary), he should have attained a degree of suppleness, balance and impulsion (controlled energy). In addition to the requirements for the previous levels, rider and horse are evaluated for accuracy. In the United States, horses must perform a half-pirouette at the walk and a simple change of leg (changing the leg that leads). In Great Britain, horses must be able to execute the collected trot and canter, 10-meter (11 yard) circles at canter, and medium trot and canter.

The Third Level (Medium and Advanced Medium) tests are of medium difficulty and are designed to determine that the horse has increased suppleness, impulsion and balance. At this level, the horse must perform the collected walk, trot and canter; medium trot and canter; extended trot and canter; counter canter; rein-back; half-pass and renvers (haunches-in) at the trot; and voltes (six meter/seven yard circles) at the trot. Competition in Great Britain also requires single flying changes, which are performed by the horse changing legs in the air between strides at the canter.

At the Fourth Level (Advanced) the horse is expected to always remain reliably at the bit. He must show complete obedience, relaxation, collection and extension, and he must demonstrate a high degree of suppleness, balance, impulsion and lightness. He should be able to trot zig-zags at half-pass (a lateral movement), canter serpentine with flying changes, perform half-pirouettes at the canter and four-time flying changes. He is now ready to move on to the international test levels.

The Prix St Georges is the first FEI level of competition. This test and the next two levels are designed to be progressive preparation for the Grand Prix tests. The Prix St Georges represents the medium stage of training and is comprised of exercises that show the horse's submission to all the demands of classical equitation. The horse must be able to counter-canter serpentines or circles of about 15 meters (16.5 yards) and canter zig-zags at half-pass with flying changes.

The Intermediate I is a test of relatively advanced standard. It is a midway point between the Prix St Georges and the Intermediate II.

The Intermediate II is an advanced test, the object of which is to ease the path for horses on their way to, but not yet ready for, the Grand Prix and its fundamental 'airs and graces' of the Classical High School.

The Grand Prix is a test of the highest standard, requiring almost seven minutes to perform. As defined by the FEI, it is a competition of artistic equitation illustrating 'the horse's perfect lightness characterized by the total absence of resistance and complete development of impulsion. The test includes all the school paces and all the fundamental airs of Classical High School.' These include the collected, extended and free walk; the collected, medium and extended trot and canter; the passage, which is a highly elevated, highly cadenced trot; the piaffe (a collected trot in place); half-passes at the trot and canter; pirouettes at the walk and canter; and flying changes of lead every second stride (nine changes) and every stride (15 changes). The test is worth a total of 430 points, and it usually takes a score of 70 percent or better to win in top-level international competition.

The Grand Prix Special has the same standard as the Grand Prix but is slightly shorter and more concentrated, with particular emphasis placed on transitions. Only the top 12 riders from the Grand Prix compete in the Special.

In keeping with the regal appearance of the horse, the rider is required to conform to a dress code. In the Training through Fourth levels, riders must wear a short riding coat with ties, choker or stock tie, breeches or jodhpurs, boots or jodhpurs boots, a hunt cap or riding hat with hard shell, derby or top hat. For competition above the Fourth Level, the dress code requires a dark tailcoat with top hat, or a black jacket with bowler hat, and white or light-colored breeches, hunting stock, gloves, black riding boots and spurs.

An English-type saddle is required at all levels. For Training, First, Second and Third Level tests, the AHSA requires that the rider use a plain snaffle bridle and a regular cavesson, a dropped noseband, a flash noseband (a combination of a cavesson noseband and a dropped noseband attachment), crescent noseband or a crossed

Above: **The judge looks at the horse's paces, movement, carriage, suppleness, attitude, energy and muscular development, as shown in his basic paces or gaits, his acceptance of the bit and of the rider's weight and aids. The judge also looks at how well each movement is executed and whether it is performed in exactly the right place.**

Below: **An all-purpose saddle. The pads are typical of those used in dressage.**

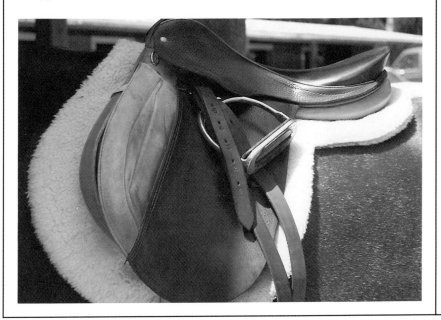

Above: In competitive jumping, horse and rider must follow a predetermined course over a variety of jumps within a given time limit.

noseband. Except for the crescent noseband and buckles, the noseband must be made entirely of leather or a leather-like material. The same type of equipment, with the addition of a simple double bridle, is permitted in the Fourth and AHSA international test levels. In FEI competition, a simple double bridle is used.

Acceptable bits for dressage include the following:
1. Ordinary snaffle with single-jointed mouthpiece.
2. Ordinary snaffle with double-jointed mouthpiece.
3. Racing snaffle.
4. Snaffle, with cheeks and with or without keepers; or snaffle, without cheeks.
5. Snaffle with upper cheeks only.
6. Unjointed snaffle.
7. Snaffle with cheeks, such as a D-ring or other ordinary snaffle.
8. Half-moon curb bit.
9. Curb bit with curved cheeks and port.
10. Curb bit with loops for lip strap on cheek and with port.
11. Curb bit with port and sliding mouthpiece (Weymouth).
12. Curb chain.
13. Lip strap.
14. Dr Bristol.
15. Fulmer.
16. French snaffle.

JUMPING

To the uninitiated, the words horse show conjure up an image of beautiful horses soaring effortlessly over high hedges. While show jumping is only a small part of what horse shows are all about, it is certainly one of the most spectacular events to watch, and, for the general public, jumping *as a sport* is much easier to follow than other equestrian events. If a horse knocks a pole off the fence, he will be penalized, whereas the subtleties of dressage figures may well be lost on many people. Its sheer drama, combined with its accessibility, has made show jumping immensely popular.

Jumping as an organized sport has existed for well over a hundred years. Although the first 'leaping contests,' as they were then called, were most likely held at horse and agricultural fairs of the early nineteenth century, the first 'official' jumping contest was held in Paris in 1866. Most early competitions were over a single high jump (bars with a hedge) or a single broad jump over water (also with a hedge as a takeoff). Those horses of a hundred years ago made some incredible leaps, especially considering that the riders leaned *back* as the horse took the fence. In 1884, at the National Horse Show in

Above: Fans of jumping consider it the most exciting, most dramatic of all equestrian sports–and it's easy to see why. Here, Joe Fargis on Mill Pearl executes a perfect jump. Fargis won the individual show jumping event at the 1984 Olympic Games in Los Angeles.

Above: Jumping involves a series of highly coordinated movements in which the weight of the horse is transferred back and forth between the forelegs and the hindquarters. As this causes a considerable shift in the center of gravity, the horse must have a high degree of muscle control so that he does not fall or lose his balance.

New York, a horse named Leo jumped 1.98 meters (6 feet, 6 inches). By 1891, the record was 2.16 meters (7 feet, 1 inch). Heatherbloom, a Thoroughbred, jumped 2.40 meters (7 feet, 10.5 inches) at Richmond, Virginia in competition and later jumped 2.49 meters (8 feet, 2 inches) while schooling at home, a height that would be record-breaking today if it were performed under FEI conditions. In the past, good jumpers belonged to almost any breed, but in recent years some version of a warmblood-Thoroughbred cross is beginning to predominate. A jumper must have powerful muscles, especially in the hindquarters, a long, free neck and perfect control over his muscles so that he can rapidly change direction in a restricted area. A jumper must also be able to change pace and gait quickly and be able to respond immediately to the slightest signal from the rider. In addition to their physical aptitude, the best show jumpers are intelligent, courageous and imbued with a competitive spirit.

Training a show jumper requires a great deal of time and patience. The relationship between horse and rider must be built on trust, eventually developing into complete understanding. The rider must learn to anticipate the horse's reaction. Both horse and rider must have a keen sense of timing and control.

Training a horse to jump often begins with teaching it to step over a rail on the ground. From there, the horse progresses to jumping over very small fences at a trot and then a canter, often from a longe line. Gradually, the size, as well as the complexity, of the obstacles is increased. As a general rule of thumb, it takes two years for a horse to advance from a rail on the ground to jumping a medium-sized course. It will take another two years before he is ready for Grand Prix (the highest level) competition, assuming he has the innate ability to jump over such high fences. Most jumpers' careers fall between the ages of nine and 15. Before the age of nine, a horse typically lacks the necessary experience, and after 15, the natural aging process weakens his ability.

Show jumping is designed to be progressive. In Germany, for example, competitions are classified as 'L,' 'M' or 'S' for *Leicht, Mittel* and *Schwer*–easy, medium and difficult. The French system is based on the horse's age, while British competitions follow a lettered grading system based on prize monies earned. The AHSA in the United States operates under a system similar to the British, although the first level of competition, called the 'Warm-up' or 'Schooling,' earns no prize money and is purely for the experience of jumping lots of small courses (1.07 meters/3 feet, 6 inches). When a horse has mastered the small course, he advances to the Preliminary Jumper section and 1.22- to 1.37-meter (4-foot to 4-foot, 6-inch) fences. A Preliminary Jumper is a horse that has won less than $2500 in prize money. A horse may stay in the Preliminary section for a full year. Then, after winning $2500, he moves up to the next level–Intermediate. Fences in the Intermediate section average 1.37 to 1.52 meters (4 feet, 6 inches to 5 feet). When a horse has earned a total of $5000, he moves up the Open section. This is the turning point in a horse's career. If he is good, he can compete in FEI events. There are also AHSA competitions for juniors and amateurs, the net result being that just about any rider can find an appropriate level of competition.

Jumping competitions vary between those that emphasize speed over a course and those that emphasize precision over the larger obstacles. In the event of a tie, there will be a jump-off, in which horse and rider repeat the course. In some cases, the obstacles have been raised or widened and the course shortened.

Competitions throughout most of the world are scored in the same way. Four faults are given for any knockdown of a fence, whether by the front or hind legs, and for any foot in a water jump or on the tape marking its limits. Three faults are given for the first refusal to jump a fence, six for the second, and elimination for the third. Eight faults are given if either the horse or rider falls. Time faults are incurred at one-quarter fault per second over the allotted time.

Above: Both horse and rider must have a keen sense of timing and exhibit perfect control.

COMBINED TRAINING

A combined training event includes two or three tests from dressage, endurance and jumping. The ultimate combined training event is the three-day event in the Olympic Games (which is explained below). The AHSA conducts a three-day event, a two-day event, a horse trial and a combined test.

The AHSA's three-day event follows the same procedures as the Olympic competition. The two-day event is also comprised of three distinct tests, this time carried out over a period of two instead of three days. The event begins with a dressage competition, followed by a jumping test, and concluding with an endurance test consisting of four phases. Phases A and C are road and track tests, phase B is a steeplechase, and phase D is a cross-country test.

A horse trial is a condensed version of the three-day event. Over the course of one day, there is a dressage test, a cross-country test and a jumping test. A combined test is comprised of two of the three tests of a horse trial.

All of these tests are offered at various levels of competition.

THE THREE-DAY EVENT

The three-day event has its origins in the military, and though it has long since lost its connection to the military, the event is still based on it original principles: a multiphase test of a horse's endurance and versatility. On the first day, the horse and rider perform a dressage test of moderate difficulty. The grueling second day tests the horse's speed and endurance, including a steeplechase

Above: **Molly Bliss and Dare Devil confront a water obstacle on the cross-country jumping component of the three-day event.**

and a cross-country jumping course. The event culminates with a stadium jumping course of moderate difficulty.

The three-day event is spread out in space, as well as time. The endurance phase of the event must be held in an area at least the size of a golf course, and many spectators follow along the course. In fact, 'eventing' often turns into a day in the country, complete with picnic baskets, small children and dogs (on a leash, of course).

The three-day event is an Olympic competition that follows FEI rules, but the sport has various levels and modifications that allow the novice to participate. There are also one- and two-day events that focus on jumping and dressage while considerably modifying the endurance element.

On the international level, the three-day event begins with dressage test set up according to FEI standards. The test is of moderate difficulty and includes working, medium and extended gaits; half-passes at the trot; and serpentines with counter-canter. In all, 20 separate movements, each worth 10 points, are performed. Including marks for paces, impulsion, submission and position of the rider, the test is worth 240 points. As in regular dressage, 10s are rarely given, so a score of 70 percent is considered quite good, especially hen one considers that the horses are trained to excel at speed and endurance. In the dressage ring, these horses must call upon a

completely different set of skills as they calmly and exquisitely carry out subtle movements at slow gaits before a large crowd.

The second day is the heart of the event, testing, as the FEI rules explain, the 'speed, endurance and jumping ability of the true cross-country horse when it is well-trained and brought to the peak of condition.' The rider's knowledge of pace and judgement of his horse's ability and condition is also evaluated. The endurance part of the event is divided into four components. The first phase is a road and track test of about six kilometers (four miles), performed at a trot or a slow canter, averaging 220 meters (240 yards) per minute. The second phase is a steeplechase of approximately 10 fences to be jumped at 690 meters (755 yards) per minute. The third phase, like the first, is a road and track test of 13.8 kilometers (eight miles). The two road and track tests together should equal 16.06 to 19.8 kilometers (10 to 12.5 miles). The final phase is cross-country jumping over a course of up to 7970 meters (5 miles) performed at the gallop, at a speed of 570 meters (620 yards) per minute. There are 28 to 32 varied obstacles. Fences should be no higher than 1.2 meters (3 feet, 11 inches), ditches no wider than 3.5 meters (11 feet, 6 inches), and banks no more than four meters (13 feet, 2 inches).

The road and track phases are basically ways of moving the horses from point A to point B while providing a warm up and cool down

Above: **The determination can be seen on Anne Riley's face as she and Mr Tambourine Man make a seemingly effortless jump.**

Above: **The idea of racing horses over a course with obstacles originated among Irish and English fox hunters in the mid-eighteenth century. Today, steeplechasing is popular worldwide, as a sport in itself as well as part of the three-day event.**

for the steeplechase. The steeplechase is fairly straightforward and the top horses usually score the maximum points. The final phase, the cross-country jump, draws thousands of spectators with its ingenious obstacles. Though a fence of only 1.2 meters (3 feet, 11 inches) may not sound like much to a show jumper, the fences are designed with big drops, ditches, and banks. The high point of the three-day event, the cross-country phase tests not only the horse's physical ability with its difficult obstacles but also the horse's spirit and desire to win.

Each obstacle on the cross-country or steeplechase course is surrounded by a penalty zone of 30 meters (33 yards) in depth, and it is only within this area that penalties are scored. Refusals are penalized 20 points for the first occurrence, 40 for the second and elimination for the third. Falls of the horse or rider or both are penalized 60 points, but the second fall on the steeplechase and the third on the cross-country eliminate.

The endurance phase is demanding but in no way cruel to the horse. The horses have been prepared to handle this event and are carefully monitored by veterinarians throughout the event. All horses are given a complete veterinary exam prior to the final competition—the stadium jumping. Indeed, the purpose of the stadium jumping is to show that the horse has the 'suppleness, energy and obedience' to perform the jumps *after* a severe test of endurance.

Clearly, the horse capable of successfully executing the three-day event is no ordinary horse, as the qualities required are many and varied. Above all, the horse must be sound and possess the predisposition to stay sound. Second, the temperament of the ideal three-day horse is courageous and resourceful but also compliant. Finally, the horse must be fairly swift and a good jumper. The desired characteristics may be found in any breed; many Thoroughbreds typically possess the courage and nerve that is so vital for this spectacular event.

Training the three-day horse is difficult and time-consuming. The process of conditioning the horse takes time. Moreover, both horse and rider must master four different disciplines: dressage, steeplechase, cross-country jumping and show jumping. Each is distinct and separate from the others, as illustrated by the need for different equipment. Each discipline uses a different seat and length of stirrup, and many riders will use a different saddle or bridle. Of course, each involves its own strategy.

HUNTER

Shows for hunters are extremely popular in the eastern United States, and in testimony to their popularity, the AHSA offers nine different sections for the hunter: Regular Conformation, Green Conformation, Hunter Breeding, Regular Working, Green Working, Hunter Pony, Junior Hunter, Amateur Owner Hunter, Children's Hunter and Adult Amateur Hunter.

In the Hunter division, horses are judged on the basis of performance and soundness, and in some cases, on conformation, suitability or manners. For the first two years of competition, a horse may be shown as a Green horse. A horse may then move into the Regular section.

Soundness is judged by jogging the horse while the rider is dismounted. Judging for performance can take place in a ring or on an outside course. Judges evaluate the horse's pace, which should be an 'even hunting pace,' and jumping style, combined with the horse's way of moving over the course.

The obstacles on the course simulate what would naturally be found in a hunting field, such as a natural post and rail, brush, stone wall, white board fence or gate, hedge and chicken coop. Every course must have at least four different types of obstacles. The height of the obstacles varies with the class (Amateur, Ladies Side Saddle and so on), ranging from .8 to 1.4 meters (2 feet, 9 inches to 4 feet 6, inches).

Knocking down an obstacle (an obstacle is considered knocked down when its height is lowered) and disobediences, such as refusing to jump an obstacle or bolting on the course, are penalized. A horse will be eliminated for a third refusal, jumping an obstacle before it is reset, bolting from the ring, jumping an obstacle not included in the course or failing to keep the proper course. Falls of horse or rider will also result in elimination.

Riders must wear conservative coats, breeches and hunting cap. In the Ladies Side Saddle class, women must wear a black or dark blue riding habit. Formal attire classes are rare.

In the Hunter Breeding division, horses are judged on conformation, quality, substance, soundness and suitability or, in the case of sires and dams, apparent ability to produce hunters.

The Hunter Pony, Children's Hunter and Junior Hunter sections are for riders under 18 years of age.

ENDURANCE RIDING

Endurance riding is a relatively new but fast growing sport. It appeals to both competitive equestrians and to people who enjoy the outdoors, especially riding trails in new areas. An endurance ride is a cross-country competition of 50 (80 kilometers) or more miles. Rides of 50 miles (80 kilometers) must be completed in 12 hours or less. Rides of at least 25 miles (40 kilometers) but not more than 35 miles (50 kilometers) are classified as limited distance rides.

The rides are controlled by equine veterinarians who monitor the horse, before, during and after the event. Several times during an endurance ride there will be veterinary checks. Pulse recovery is an important factor used to determine the condition of the horse. The ride veterinarians will set the pulse criteria and announce it before the start of the ride. The horses are also monitored for any other physical reactions including lameness, dehydration, cardiac

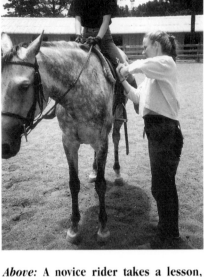

Above: **A novice rider takes a lesson, with an eye toward competition in the Children's Hunter division. One of the first things she must learn is the proper position for the stirrups.**

Above: **Arabians excel at endurance riding, but typically the horses that compete in performance, do not compete in halter. Remington Steele, however, is the only US and Canadian Top Ten Halter Stallion in the history of the breed to successfully complete the 100-mile Tevis Cup endurance ride. Here, Remington Steele navigates Cougar Rock on the Tevis trail.**

stress and so on. If a horse is not in optimum condition to continue, the veterinarians will pull him from the ride. The first horse to finish, providing he is completely sound, is considered the over-all winner. Among the top 10 finishers, a special award is presented to the horse in Best Condition, and a token prize goes to each horse and rider who finish—which is no small accomplishment, for their motto is 'To finish is to win.'

The course for an endurance ride varies with the topography of the area. Some are on flat or gently rolling land; others cover mountainous terrain with steep ascents or descents. Riders are allowed to dismount and lead their horse at any time. Footing can vary from the shoulder of paved roads to grass, sand, gravel, dirt, slab rock or old forest trails. When laying out a course, the ride manager attempts to avoid obvious hazards such as deep bogs and sheer cliffs; however, an endurance horse is expected to take in stride most natural obstacles.

Temperature, climate, footing and terrain will determine the speed at which the horses can travel. A tough hilly trail is actually easier on the horse than a flat open road that encourages too fast a pace.

There are also multi-day rides. These rides, which are often held on historic trails, are usually 50 to 60 miles (80 to 97 kilometers) a day in length and may be conducted over a period of four to six days. These are often point to point with ride camp moving each night. A rider may enter and compete each day as if it were a separate event.

To be successful at endurance riding, the rider must understand his horse completely. He must be able to tell when his horse is feeling fatigued or showing signs of discomfort. Above all, he should understand when it is time to slow the pace or, if necessary, stop. Success depends also on a horse's training and conditioning. Only a very fit, sound horse can compete. A ride is often the culmination of several months of preparation.

Any breed of horse can compete in endurance riding, but the sport is dominated by Arabians and Half Arabians. Thoroughbreds, Morgans, Quarter Horses and other western breeds also do well.

The most famous endurance ride is the Tevis Cup (now called the Western States Trail Ride), which follows a route used by the Pony Express, from Tahoe City, Nevada to Auburn California. Over the course of the ride, conditions vary from 100-degree Fahrenheit (38-degree Celsius) heat in El Dorado Canyon to icy wind and snow in

Above: Steve Sloan and Azul prepare for a competitive trail ride. Less rigorous than endurance riding, competitive trail riding covers from 15 to 40 miles (24 to 64 km) instead of 50 miles (80 km).

Above: Competitive trail riding is a popular sport, providing the participants with sunshine as well as fun times with friends and, of course, their horses. And when it's over everyone feels like a winner.

the Sierra Nevada mountain passes. Other well known rides include the Old Dominion Ride in Virginia, the Purina Race of Champions in Colorado and the Golden Horseshoe Ride in England. The latter is a two-day ride covering 75 miles (120 kilometers). Australia has its own famous two-day ride—the Great Two-Day Endurance Race—in Queensland, which covers 200 miles (322 kilometers) the first day and 50 miles (80 kilometers) the next.

Endurance rides in the United States are conducted under the rules of the American Endurance Ride Conference, which was organized in 1971 as a sanctioning and record-keeping body. Its first year AERC sanctioned just 24 rides, but by 1988 the number had grown to 600. The Fédération Equestre Internationale recognized endurance riding as an official international equestrian sport in 1985, and the American Horse Shows Association administers international endurance participation.

COMPETITIVE TRAIL RIDING

Competitive trail riding is similar to, but less stressful than, endurance riding. The distances covered are less, ranging from 15 to 40 miles (24 to 64 km) instead of 50 miles (80 kilometers) or more, and speed is not an issue. The ride must be completed within a stated period of time, with penalties given for completing a race too soon. Competitive trail rides are *not* races. The winners are determined according to points awarded for Soundness (40 percent), Condition (40 percent), Manners (15 percent) and Way of Going (5 percent). Judges are posted along the trail and at the finish. As with endurance riding, there are veterinary checks along the way to assure that all the horses are fit.

Competitive trail riding is a weekend sport, popular with people who enjoy spending time outdoors and with their horses. In many ways, it is a social gathering, in which people can relax and have fun camping with old friends and new acquaintances.

Competitive trail riding is not recognized by the AHSA.

EQUITATION

One of the most popular divisions in the AHSA is the Equitation Division. Subdivided into Hunter, Saddle, and Stock Seat, Equitation is for riders under 18 years of age. The rider not the horse is judged. However, all elements work together, so strategy, showmanship, an appropriate mount and the judge's personal preference in equestrian style all come into play. Competitors usually rely on the assistance of a trainer, as they prepare for the season as well as on the day of a show.

In the Hunter Seat section, riders should have a workmanlike appearance and give the impression that they are in 'complete control should any emergency arise.' The eyes should be up and the shoulders back. While at the walk, sitting trot and canter, the rider should position himself a couple of degrees in front of the vertical. At the posting trot, the gallop and while jumping, the rider should be inclined forward. Attire should be tweed or other conservative solid coat, breeches, jodhpurs and boots. Hunter Seat is a prelude to FEI and Olympic competitions.

The course must include at least six obstacles. In the lower classes, obstacles cannot exceed .9 meters (3 feet), while in championship classes obstacles cannot exceed 1.07 meters (3 feet, 6 inches).

In the Saddle Seat Equitation section, riders should be positioned in an efficient and comfortable manner that can be sustained at any gait for any length of time. Conservative attire is required. Informal dress, providing it is of a conservative color, is permitted in Saddle-bred Pleasure classes.

In the Stock Seat Equitation section, riders are judged on the basis of seat, hands, performance, appearance of horse and rider, and suitability of horse to rider. The rider should always appear comfortable, relaxed and flexible. The feet should be placed in the stirrups with the weight on ball of the foot. The heels should be lower than the toes. Arms are held in a straight line with the body. Only one hand is permitted to hold the reins, and that arm must be bent at the elbow. The hand not holding the reins may be in any position, providing it is relaxed and kept out of the way of the horse and equipment. The rider must be able to keep the horse in good form at consistent gaits and control the horse under adverse conditions.

COMBINED DRIVING

Above: **The dressage component of combined driving follows the same format as ridden dressage. The test is conducted in an arena over a course that is driven from memory.**

The first known equestrian sport was one that involved a horse in harness—chariot racing. In the twentieth century, that ancient sport no longer exists, but it has been resurrected in a new form—combined driving. This new activity is a test of driving versatility and is patterned roughly after the three-day event.

Combined driving consists of three different types of competitions that take place over three days, or four days if there are numerous competitors. A different vehicle may be used for the different competitions, but the same four horses must be driven for the entire competition. The first component, Competition A, is dressage and presentation. Dressage is held in an arena 40 by 100 meters (44 by 110 yards) and marked with letters like ridden dressage. The test, which takes about 19 minutes, must be driven from memory. The driver must demonstrate accuracy, horsemanship, and control, as well as the horses' paces and movement. Required paces are the walk and the working, collected and

Above: A four-in-hand in action. Driving is a true team effort, involving three individual human personalities and four equine personalities.

extended trots. Figures performed include circles and serpentines. The horses must also halt and reinback. Scoring is identical to ridden dressage.

The presentation element of Competition A evaluates the turnout by judging the cleanliness, condition and general appearance of the horses, vehicle, driver, grooms and harness.

Competition B, the marathon, tests the fitness, stamina and training of the horses and the judgement of pace and horsemastership of the driver. The marathon is also divided into sections. Section A is done at the trot (15 kilometers at 15 kmph/9 miles at 9 mph); Section B at the walk (1200 meters at 7 kmph/1300 yards at 4 mph); Section C at the fast trot (5 kilometers at 18 kmph/3 miles at 11 mph); Section D is the same as Section B; and Section E, like section C, is done at the trot. Section E, however, covers a greater distance, 10 kilometers at 15 kmph (6 miles at 9 mph). This section is the core of the marathon, as it includes seven or eight difficult obstacles, or hazards, that must be negotiated against the clock. With the exception of the walking sections, the other sections, may include natural hazards, such as gates, sharp turns, water and steep hills. Sections B and D are followed by a compulsory 10-minute rest period, when the horses will be given a veterinary check.

Competition C is an obstacle course, the object of which is to test the fitness, obedience, and suppleness of the horse after the marathon as well as the skill and competence of the driver. The course

covers 500 to 800 meters (547 to 875 yards) in length, with up to 20 cones spaced only slightly wider than the vehicle's wheel track. Each displacement of a cone is penalized five points. Competitors start in the reverse order of their standings and must negotiate the course at a minimum speed of 21 kmph (13 mph).

Training a horse to drive begins the same as any horse's early training. In fact, many horses are far along in saddle training before they are ever hitched to a vehicle. Typically, training begins on a longe line, progressing gradually to driving on long reins, with the 'driver' walking behind the horse. When the horse is accustomed to moving about in this manner, the harness is introduced ever so slowly, only a piece at a time. A green horse can be easily frightened by a harness, particularly the crupper that goes under the tail and the breeching that touches the hind legs, so it is crucial that this stage of the process in handled with care. Once the horse has become used to the harness, he must learn to pull something—a concept which will be altogether foreign to him. This, too, must be taught gradually, beginning with a small, light object, such as car wheel or a log, and bit-by-bit moving on to heavier objects.

The preliminary lessons learned, the horse is ready to be introduced to a simple, long-shafted, two-wheeled vehicle. Again, the entire process should be taken step-by-step. When the horse has accepted the vehicle, he must then learn to work as part of a pair pulling a large, four-wheeled vehicle. By this time, the horse has a

Above: **Driving is designed to test the fitness, obedience and suppleness of the horse(s) while testing the skill and competence of the driver.**

Above: **Vaulting is the sport of gymnastics on horseback. A relatively new discipline, vaulting is gaining popularity around the world.**

good understanding of what driving is all about and as training becomes a variation on a theme, the transition from one pair to two should go fairly smoothly. When the horse is comfortable with a four-in-hand (two pairs), he can be introduced to other, more exotic kinds of vehicles, such as the tandem (one horse in front of the other) or unicorn (two wheeler and one leader).

For competition, there are two basic ways of harnessing and bitting the team. The traditional 'English' harness consists of a regular horse collar and a regular driving bit with a curb chain. The position of the reins can be adjusted based on the degree of severity desired. In the 'Hungarian' harness, the horse wears a breastplate and a snaffle, usually with double rings. Driving techniques are almost as varied. There is the classic English and German style, in which all four reins are held in the left hand. The right hand is used to lengthen and shorten the reins by making loops, which are caught under the right thumb and released gradually as required. This method works well for managing very sharp, slow turns. A very different method for driving is based on the old American stagecoach driver approach–holding two reins in each hand. Regardless of the method used, each one requires a great deal of training and practice to achieve the accuracy to negotiate obstacles at speed and the finesse to perform dressage.

ROADSTER

Roadster competitions highlight the trotting skill of the standard or standard bred-type horses. Horses and ponies perform the trot at three speeds: a slow 'jog trot,' a fast 'road gait' and 'at speed,' a full-speed trot. Roadsters are shown to a bike or wagon, as well as under saddle. Ponies, however, are not shown under saddle. Competition begins as the horse enters the ring clockwise at a jog trot. The horse then shows at the road gait, next he turns counter clockwise at the jog trot, again shows at the road gait and finally trot 'at speed.' Horses go 'at speed' in both directions. Judges are looking for animation, brilliance and 'show ring presence' when the horse is executing a jog trot or road gait.

VAULTING

Vaulting is the most unusual of all equestrian sports. Instead of breeches and boots, the 'riders' wear leotards and soft-soled gymnastic slippers as they perform gymnastic exercises on the back of a trotting or cantering horse. The horse, which is controlled by a longe line, wears a leather vaulting surcingle with a ring on top to which a strap is attached. There are hand grips on either side of the surcingle and loops farther down to hold the vaulter's feet during some of the more spectacular Cossack-style figures.

Though there are numerous informal events, there are also national and international competitions sponsored under AHSA and FEI rules and regulations. These competitions feature a team event, individual men's and women's events, and a *pas de deux*.

The team competition begins with six compulsory exercises performed individually as the horse circles the arena: the basic seat, the flag, the mill, the flank, the free stand and the scissors. Then, the team as a whole performs a Kur—a five-minute freestyle program set to music, highlighting the technique, teamwork and creativity of the team. All eight members of the team must perform in the Kur, but no more than three vaulters may be on the horse at one time. The Kur is judged on degree of difficulty (height off the horse, demands of suppleness and stretch, complications of movements), composition (transitions, artistic development of program and artistic interpretation of the music) and performance (mechanics, form, balance and consideration for the horse).

The individual events follow the same format as the team event, except that the Kur is only one minute long instead of five.

The *pas de deux* event is performed by the vaulters and consists of two separate Kur exercises. The first Kur (Kur I) is a one-minute free-style routine that emphasizes synchronous mirror-image exercises. Kur II is a two-minute free-style routine with no special requirements or limitations.

The horses used for vaulting can be any breed. Quarter Horses, Morgans and Appaloosas are frequently seen in the ring. In Germany, where the sport has quite a following, retired dressage horses are often used for beginning vaulters because their training has made them more flexible and supple. Gentle ponies make good mounts for children entering the sport. Vaulting horses must be at least six years of age.

WESTERN

Western competitions simulate the performance of the horse as used in a working, western environment—on a ranch, riding over trails and walking. The Western Division of the AHSA is divided into the Stock Section, the Trail Horse Section, the Pleasure Horse Section and the Western Riding Horse Section. The competition takes place in an arena.

In the Stock Section, the horse and rider perform a reining test, beginning the workout with a figure eight at a lope once or twice. The horse must make two flying changes of lead during each figure eight. After the figure eights, the horse and rider must go to the end of the arena, turn and run the full length of the arena to a straight, sliding stop, turn away from the rail and run to the center of the arena and make a straight, sliding stop. The rider must then back the horse in exactly the opposite direction in a straight line for 3 to 4.6

Above: **Western competition simulates the performance of a horse in a working, western environment–on a ranch, riding over trails and walking.**

meters (10 to 15 feet). The horse must then be brought forward, stopped, and with his weight on his hindquarters and with his legs in position, make a half turn once in each direction.

The second component of the Stock competition is cow work, in which a cow is turned loose in the arena. The horse and rider must try to turn the cow at least once each way against the fence. The cow must then be taken to the center of the ring and circled once each way. Horses are awarded 60 to 80 points for the reining test and 60 to 80 points for the cow work, for a total of 160 points. Falls of horse or rider may be penalized at the judge's discretion.

In the Trail Horse Section, horses are required to work over and through obstacles. The course has between six and eight obstacles, and the horse must perform such things as negotiating a gate, carrying objects from one part of the arena to another, riding through water, over logs or simulated brush, riding down into and up out of a ditch without lunging or jumping, crossing a bridge, backing through obstacles, sidepassing, mounting and dismounting from either side, and any type of obstacle a horse would naturally encounter on a trail. Horses must demonstrate a walk, jog and a lope as they negotiate the trail.

Left and above: **After the show is over, the winners proudly display their awards.**

Entries are evaluated on responsiveness, willingness and general attitude, and a horse will be penalized for any delay in approaching an obstacle. Manners compose 70 percent of the score; appointments, equipment, neatness 20 percent; and conformation 10 percent.

In the Pleasure Horse Section, horses are shown at a flat footed four-beat walk, a jog and a lope, with most emphasis placed on the walk. The judge may also ask for extended gaits. Horse and rider will be penalized for being on the wrong lead. Horses are judged on performance (60 percent), appointments (30 percent) and conformation (10 percent).

Above: During a lull in the action, participants take the opportunity to socialize with their horses.

Facing page: The beauty, athletic ability and willing temperament of the Morgan English pleasure horse is enjoyed by junior exhibitors, amateur owners and professional horsemen.

The Western Riding Horse Section tests the performance and characteristics of a good, sensible, well-mannered, free and easy moving ranch horse that can help a person perform the usual ranch chores, maneuver over trails or give a quiet, comfortable and pleasant ride in the open country through and over obstacles. Horses are shown in standard Western equipment and are judged on manners (70 percent); appointments, equipment, neatness (10 percent); and conformation (20 percent).

PARADE HORSE AND SADDLE HORSE

Parade Horse competitions are a celebration of the beauty of the horse and rider. The ideal Parade Horse is a beautiful stylish animal, displaying refinement, personality and eye appeal. Horses may be of any breed or color. Good manners are essential, both in executing gaits and in the ring. Horses must be shown with a full mane, which may be braided.

The horse is shown at an animated walk and at a parade gait. The animated walk is a graceful four-beat, straight, brisk movement. The parade gait is a straight, high-prancing movement, with a maximum speed of eight kmph (five mph). The parade gait is collected and balanced, with the hocks well under. Riders should wear a fancy cowboy suit, hat and boots that are typical of the Old West, or of American, Mexican or Spanish origin.

Competition begins as the horse enters the ring at a parade gait. He should be shown at the two required gaits, then reversed at a walk, and shown again at the two gaits. Martial music should be played whenever possible.

Horses are judged on the basis of performance, manners and conformation (75 percent) and appointments of horse and rider (25 percent). (However, in the Pinto Class, which is not an AHSA event, the breakdown is manners and conformation 50 percent, appointments 25 percent and markings 25 percent.) Faults include excessive speed, bad manners, switching tail, exaggerated opening of mouth, hard mouth, fighting the bit, halting or hesitating, and zig-zagging or sideways movement. Competitors will be disqualified for performing gaits other than the ones specified; the use of martingales, draw reins and other appliances; and any artificial change of color or markings other than mane or tail.

This division also includes saddle type horses, which may be of any color or breed. In this class, horses are shown at a walk, trot and canter. Riders may wear Western clothing and boots or colorful parade clothing. Horses are judged on the basis of performance and manners (60 percent) and conformation and soundness (40 percent).

HORSE SHOWS BY BREED

These pages: **Appaloosas. Spotted ponies were introduced to North America by Cortez in the early 1500s. The Nez Perce Indians prized these horses for their speed and toughness and established a breeding program using only the finest stallions. Today, Arab, Thoroughbred and Quarter horses are used to improve the breed.**

A number of breeds have such a popular following that some horse shows focus solely on the skills and beauty of a particular breed.

APPALOOSA

This horse's name is adapted from 'Palouse,' the name of the area in which it originated. The Palouse River drainage is an area encompassing northeast Oregon, southeast Washington and bordering the area in Idaho that was the traditional home of the Nez Perce Indian tribe. The pronunciation of the word 'palouse' became slurred to Apalouse, and eventually Appaloose, then Appaloosa. It is thought that these horses came into the possession of the Nez Perce about 1730, although the Spaniards used the horses earlier. Early fur traders coming into the area saw the horses and referred to them as the 'Nez Perce's horses.' The Nez Perce valued these horses so highly that they would not sell or trade a single animal. They are credited as the first tribe to systematically improve a breed of horses. Some writers have credited the Nez Perce Indians with the development of the breed, but the horse's ancestry actually dates back much further. It is true, however, that Chief Joseph and his tribe of Nez Perce in Eastern Washington and Northern Idaho loved their Appaloosas, and no doubt tried to breed them so that they might perpetuate the Appaloosa coloring. After the Nez Perce were defeated and placed on reservations in 1877, the horses became scattered, and it was not until the 1920s that an effort was made to re-establish the breed. An Oregon wheat rancher and horse breeder named Claude Thompson was instrumental in starting the movement to re-establish this breed. The Appaloosa Horse Club was organized in 1938 in Oregon, and now has its headquarters in Moscow, Idaho.

The first 4932 horses registered are considered the foundation stock. Since then, both parents must be registered before an offspring can be recorded. However, there is now a provision for

Above: **Riders at an Appaloosa Horse Club steeplechase. Appaloosas are also frequent competitors at Western events, as hunters and jumpers, and on endurance trails.**

Facing page: **Remington Steele—a bold, beautiful Arabian stallion. Arabians are known for their striking heads, with brilliant, expressive eyes and alert ears.**

tentative registration of an outstanding foal whose sire and dam are not registered. To be eligible, the horse must have Appaloosa breeding, have proper coloring, be of proper conformation and be of desirable type. Horses of draft type, pintos or paints are not acceptable. Horses listed with this tentative registration may become permanent if, as a sire, they can produce twelve foals of desirable type. In the case of a mare, she must produce three such foals to achieve permanent registration. Color is the most important feature in an Appaloosa. Therefore, horses may range widely in size, but are typically from 14.2 to 15.2 hands.

The registered Appaloosa horse must have mottled skin, which is most clearly seen around the lips, nostrils and genitalia. This skin will actually sunburn just like that of a fair-skinned human! It must also claim the distinctive white sclera in the eye. While not all spotted horses are Appaloosas, the five principal coat patterns that are considered in the registration of this breed are:

Leopard—Spots which are an opposite to the background color.

Spotted Blanket—A white rump and back with a dark background.

White Blanket—White overall.

Snowflake—White spots on any dark color.

Marble—Mottled all over the body.

Frost—Tiny white spots on a darker background, or vice-versa, all over the body.

Appaloosas have good legs and chests, short backs and well-shaped necks, yet their tails and manes tend to be rather sparse and fine-haired.

Appaloosas are very prominent in all types of Western riding and also compete in various Appaloosa games such as stump racing and rope racing. In addition, Appaloosas can be found in the show ring as hunters and jumpers and on endurance trails.

ARABIAN

The Arabian holds an unchallenged position of leadership in the initial development of the horse world's finest breeds and their subsequent lines. Indeed, Arabian blood has been used at one stage or another to improve the quality of nearly every major horse breed that exists! Early history tells us that kings and emperors worshipped the liver chestnut colored Arabians.

There is much speculation about the Arabian's origin, but Professor Sir William Ridgeway, who has done considerable research on the subject, suggests that the Arabian horse is a descendant of the wild Libyan horse that came from northern Africa and had been domesticated in Egypt centuries before the Christian era. Consequently, the people of North Africa have been breeding and improving the stock for many centuries.

There is also evidence of the breed's existence on the Arabian peninsula as far back as 5000 BC. There, the Arabs jealously protected the purity of its blood for centuries, certifying that no foreign

Above: **Arabians are intelligent and even-tempered animals. Constant association with their Arab masters produced horses with an extra-large, keen brain and a gentle nature.**

Arabians excel at numerous equestrian events, including Western pleasure and trail, English pleasure, dressage and endurance riding. *Facing page:* **Andy Bailey and KJ Khalata, a pure-bred Arabian mare, cross the American River on the Tevis trail.**

blood was ever introduced into the line. Today, mention of the Arabian never fails to bring out a feeling of romantic mystique, associated with the rippling sands of the Arabian desert.

The history of the wandering tribes of Bedouins is legendary. They developed a worldwide reputation as skilled horsemen and horse breeders, who held their horses in the highest esteem. For centuries, these people have depended on their horses in their everyday lives, whether to care for their flocks, to plunder neighboring areas, or to ward off the enemy in desert warfare.

In England, Arabians strongly influenced the creation of the Thoroughbred. The foundation sires of the Darley, Godolphin, and the Byerly Turk breeds were imported in the seventeenth and eighteenth centuries. The earliest account that we have of the Arabian's introduction to the United States is described by Homer Davenport in his books *Arab Horse* and *My Quest of the Arab Horse*. According to his account, the Arabian stallion Ranger was imported to America about 1765. This horse is said to have sired the gray horse that George Washington rode during the American Revolutionary War. Commander JG Elliot of the US Navy imported a consignment of both stallions and mares in 1838, and in 1856, Keene Richards imported two stallions and two mares. During and after the Civil War, however, Arabian blood became mixed with the American Saddlebred. In 1893, more Arabians were imported for the World

Above: **A woman and her Arabian enjoy a scenic cross-country ride.**

Columbian Exposition in Chicago. Around the turn of the century, Davenport himself was one of the largest importers of Arabians. In 1906, he brought 26 head–and later many more–directly from the Arabian desert to his farm at Morris Plains, New Jersey.

Pure bred Arabian horses are of solid color, bay, brown, gray, chestnut and sometimes white or black. White in the face and on the legs is common, but spots on the body are objectionable. One of the Arabian's outstanding characteristics is its beautiful head and neck, bright clear eyes, well placed ears and large nostrils. The 'dished' shape of the face below the eyes is another important trademark. Their pasterns are long and strong; their feet are slightly larger than other breeds of comparative size. The Egyptian Arabian, regrettably, is no longer bred by the tribesmen in Arabia. This type tends to be slightly finer boned, and have–if such is possible–an even more refined and graceful head.

Not a large horse, the Arabian usually stands 14.1 to 15.2 hands high, but its physical endurance parallels no other breed in the world. Its most popular uses today are in Western and English riding, and as a show horse. There are probably more Arabian horse shows today than those of any other single breed. Horses are judged on conformation, as well as performance. The performance classes are many and varied, including English pleasure, hunter, jumper, park horse, western and driving. With contests in pole bending, barrel racing, cutting and reining, these shows are fun to watch as well as dramatic. There is even a class for native costumes, in which the riders wear long, flowing capes and scarves while adorning their horses in colorful desert regalia. Half-Arabians and Anglo-Arabians are permitted to enter certain competitions.

A four-year-old Connemara mare *(right)* and a Connemara stallion *(above)*. In the past the Connemara was used for farm work, but today it is used primarily as a riding pony and is especially suitable for young riders. If crossed with a larger horse, the Connemara can produce good jumpers capable of excelling in competition.

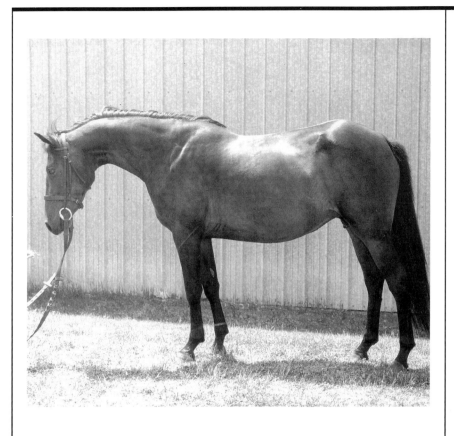

CONNEMARA

The only pony native to Ireland, the Connemara boasts the beauty of the Arabian, as well as the strength and hardiness of the Mountain Pony. The breed has been influenced by Arabian, Thoroughbred and Fjord stock. It is found in the wild along the northeast coast of County Galway in Ireland, but can quickly be tamed into a gentle, well-behaved animal in a matter of a few days. The Connemara Stud Book was established in 1924.

To compete in an AHSA show, a Connemara must be registered with the American Connemara Pony Society and/or the Connemara Pony Breeders Society (CPBS) of Galway, Ireland, or any society recognized by the CPBS.

Connemaras are shown as typical hunters. Emphasis is placed on manners and an appropriate way of going. In the breeding and in-hand classes, horses are judged according to the breed standard. Weaknesses in type that can be passed to offspring are considered serious faults. Entries are shown in-hand at the walk and trot.

Performance classes conform to the rules for Hunters. In the Versatile Connemara Class, horses are shown in three of the four following events: pleasure driving, hunter pleasure, western pleasure, and jumping over obstacles less than .9 meters (three feet) in height.

Usually standing no more than 14.2 hands, the Connemara excels in jumping events, often outjumping horses of 16 and 17 hands. The

Above and right: The size and temperament of Hackney ponies make them ideally suited for indoor racing. The 'jockey' is a mechanical device known as SuperJock.

Facing page: In contrast to the Connemaras pictured on the previous page, this pony is a work horse, used for pulling a tinker's wagon through the Irish countryside.

great Connemara jumpers included Little Squire, who stood 13.2 hands–average for the breed–but consistently cleared 2.13-meter (seven-foot) jumps, while carrying a 72-kg (160-pound) rider. Another horse, Nugget, stood 15 hands. At the International Horse Show at the Olympic in London in 1935, he cleared 2.2 meters (7 feet, 2 inches) to win the event. The great Connemara jumper, Dundrum, won the jumping competition at the Royal Dublin Horse Show for four straight years, competing against the finest jumpers in Europe.

His greatest year was 1963, when he won the Aga Khan trophy, the King George V trophy, plus other world class meets, and was proclaimed 'King of the World's Jumping Horses.'

HACKNEY AND HACKNEY HARNESS PONY

The Hackney Pony is a British breed derived from the Hackney, a breed that has become synonymous with the highest class of carriage horse. The Hackney's skill as a carriage horse was passed along to the Hackney Pony, which today excels at harness competi-

Above: **The National Park Service at Point Reyes National Seashore in California raises Morgan Horses. Since they are used as work horses, they are bred for size and temperament rather than for looks. Here, a Morgan is put to work as a pack horse.**

tions. For competition purposes, the maximum height of Hackney Ponies is 14.2 hands, and the maximum height of Hackney Harness Ponies is 12.2 hands. To enter an AHSA competition, a Hackney Pony must be registered with the American Hackney Horse Society or the Canadian Hackney Society.

Ponies are shown in-hand at a walk and trot. Conformation and type count for 50 percent, while performance, manners, disposition and way of going count for the remaining 50 percent.

In the conduct classes, all ponies are exhibited with a viceroy or a miniature side rail buggy of a type used for fine harness horses. Ponies are 'to be driven in the half cheek,' which means that the reins should be around the post or through the top slot. They must be shown in a sidecheck bridle with a liverpool bit.

Ponies are shown at two gaits: the park trot, a highly collected trot and 'Show Your Pony,' which is the speed that shows the pony at his best advantage. Ponies can also be shown in pairs, in tandem or four-in-hand.

Above: **A Morgan of the Morgan Horse Ranch at Point Reyes practices carrying the flag.**

MORGAN HORSE

The foundation of the Morgan breed is unique in that it traces back to a single horse. The Morgan is the only breed that is named after a singing master, as well as being the oldest distinct breed in America. Justin Morgan was a frail Vermont music teacher and composer of hymns who owned a little horse, today referred to either as 'Justin Morgan's Horse,' or simply as Justin Morgan. Foaled in 1789 and died in 1821, this animal is said to have weighed no more than 386 kg (850 pounds) and to have stood 14 hands. However, in log pulling contests he bested the strongest horses in the surrounding area most of them 182 kg (400 pounds) heavier than he! Morgan's horse was also entered in many quarter-mile races against the swiftest horses that could be found. There, too, he won every time.

Above: Morgan Horses have expressive heads, large eyes and shapely ears. Their necks should come out of an extremely well-angulated shoulder, and their bodies should be compact and well muscled. These good-looking horses are known for their stamina, vigor, adaptability and attitude.

Facing page: A woman and her Morgan Horse take a peaceful ride along the California shore.

As a stallion, because of the foresight of his owner, he was mated with the best mares, and his prepotency was so great that he was able to pass on his remarkable speed, strength, endurance and his wonderfully gentle disposition to his progeny.

There are, of course, many differences of opinion as to the ancestry of Justin Morgan's little horse. Some researchers have said that his sire was a Dutch bred stallion. Others claim to have "found' that his sire was a horse named True Briton. Here, too, there is disagreement. Some say that True Briton was a Thoroughbred, while others say that he was a Welsh Cob, and still others are sure that he was an Arabian. Those that have seen the statue of the little horse at the Morgan Horse Farm in Vermont can attest to the fact that the horse leans strongly to the Cob in appearance and conformation.

About 1870, Col Battell of Middleford, Vermont began gathering information about the Morgan Horse, and continued until his death in 1915. Interest in the history of the Morgan Horse was kept alive by the US Department of Agriculture. In 1907, Col Battell donated 400 acres near Middleford, Vermont to the US Department of Agriculture for use as a Morgan Horse farm, and the present location of the American Morgan Horse Association, Inc is in Shelburne, Vermont. The National Park Service also has a small Morgan farm at Point Reyes, California.

Above: **Descendants of the Mustangs brought to the new world by the Spanish Conquistadors were a vital component of Indian culture.**

The description of the dam of Justin Morgan, given on page 95 of Volume I of the Morgan Horse Register, is as follows: 'The dam of the Morgan horse was of the Wild Air or Wildair breed; she was of middling size, her color was a light bay, mane and tail not dark, hair on legs rather long; she was a smooth handsome traveler. Her sire was the Diamond, a thick heavy horse of middle size; he had a thick bushy mane and tail; a smooth traveler.' Dr CD Parks, having extensively researched his pedigree, concludes that: "It is reasonable to believe that the dam of Justin Morgan was three-quarters Dutch and one-quarter grade Arabian. Justin Morgan would then be five-eighths grade Arabian and three-eighths Dutch. He had the bay color, heavy black mane and tail and long hair about the fetlocks, which belonged to the Dutch horse. The horses, so far as we can determine, native to the section of Vermont where Justin Morgan produced most of his offspring, were essentially the same as those credited with producing him.'

For many years, in each succeeding generation, the blood of the Morgan was diluted. Experts consider it very unusual that through all of this, his descendants continue to inherit his characteristics, spirit, shape and intelligence so closely.

Their step is short, nervous and energetic. Their great endurance rivals that of the Arabian, and they are used primarily for English and Western riding, as well as driving, like the great Morgan jumper, ridden by General Humberto Mariles, which won a gold medal at the London Olympics in 1948. Indeed, today's Morgan can be enjoyed as a pleasure horse, a working cowboy's horse, or a show horse. Many are crossbred successfully with other breeds to make quarter-mile running horses or harness horses for racing, pleasure or show.

The AHSA conducts horse shows specifically for the Morgan Horse. In addition to conformation classes, the horse competes as a park horse, parade horse, pleasure horse, trail horse, driving horse, road hack, stock horse, cutting horse, roadster, working hunter and jumper. In the Justin Morgan Class, horses trot a half-mile in harness, next run a half-mile under saddle, then show in the ring at a walk, trot, and canter, and finally pull a 500-pound (227-kg) stone boat a distance of six feet (1.83 meters) in work harness. Each of the four elements are ranked equally at 25 percent. A horse that fails to pull the stone boat is eliminated.

MUSTANG

Descended from the horses brought to North America by the Spanish Conquistadors in the sixteenth century, the Mustang, or Spanish Mustang, takes its name from the Spanish *Mesteño*, which essentially means 'belonging to the horse raiser.' The Mesteño is, in turn, of Barb and Arabian ancestry and descended from the great war horses brought to the Iberian peninsula by the Moors in the eighth century.

Left and above: Every year the American Mustang Association holds the National Grand Championship Horse Show to highlight the skills and personality of the Mustang.

According to the records of the American Mustang Association: 'The registration requirements of the different Spanish (speaking) countries were compared with each other, then compared with that which was determined about the Spanish horses at the time of the Conquistadors. This was then compared with the work of our own American writers and artists, and personal observation. Not unexpectedly, all the sources of information agreed. The Spanish descriptions of their stock were in agreement with the requirements of the South American associations. In turn, South American requirements were the same as those characteristics described by American writers. This data is the basis for the conformation standards of the

Above: Competitors in the Paso Fino Costume Class dress to reflect the Spanish and Latin American origins of the breed.

American Mustang Association. The characteristics of an American Mustang are as follows: the height is between 13.2 and 15 hands and the weight is usually between 318 and 455 kg (700 and 1000 pounds); the build is compact, well proportioned, smooth muscled, and symmetrical; in conformation the back is short coupled, there is broad width between alert eyes, and moderate head length; the legs have good flexion, are straight, and have small to medium sized chestnuts; there is good slope to the shoulder, a deep crested neck which is shorter than most breeds, and moderate withers blending into the back; the chest is of moderate width, the rib cage is well sprung, and the barrel is deep; the hindquarters are strong, the croup is rounded, and the tail set is low; the horse shows great agility and power, is well balanced, and moves with the hindquarters well under the body weight; the American Mustang is long on endurance and intelligence and has a good, adaptable disposition. Coat color and marking patterns are varied; a Mustang may be any color, from solid to mixed combinations.'

Today's American Mustang is descended from horses that were either stolen from the Conquistadors by the Indians or escaped into the wild. By the nineteenth century, large herds of wild horses roamed the West, and it is a testament to the hardiness of this little breed that they survived. Wild herds still exist in Nevada, Oregon and the Pryor Mountains of Montana, but many Mustangs have been domesticated, and the breed has a large following. Several organizations have been established around the breed, with the Southwest Spanish Mustang Association of Finley, Oklahoma having been one of the first and still one of the most active. This association sponsors many endurance and competitive trail rides, many of which are sanctioned by the American Endurance Ride Conference (AERC). The American Mustang Association, founded in Yucaipa, California in 1962, boasts a membership in excess of 1000, and holds an annual National Grand Championship Horse Show.

PASO FINO

The Paso Fino is an elegant, refined breed known for its unique, spectacular gaits. The natural Paso Fino gait is an animated, collected walk; the Classic Fino is a smooth, four-beat lateral gait that is fast and flashy; the Paso Corto is also a four-beat gait, but with moderate speed and extension; and the Paso Largo is bold and animated, with longer extension and greater speed than the Paso Corto. In the ring, horses must also perform a smooth, unhurried canter and a slow, cadenced lope.

Paso Finos are native to Puerto Rico but are derived from the Arab, Andalusian and Barb horses that Columbus and the Moors brought to the New World. Paso Finos have medium long necks and shoulders that slope into the withers. The legs are fine boned and strong, with small, strong hoofs. Horses are slow to mature and may not reach full growth until five years of age. Paso Finos can be any

color, although bay, chestnut and black are the predominant colors.

To generate interest in the breed, competitors in the Paso Fino Costume Class wear costumes reflecting the Spanish and Latin American origins of the breed. Riders must also submit a brief essay (100 words or less) explaining the cultural significance of their costume. The essay is read as each competitor enters the ring.

QUARTER HORSE

When the Quarter Horse is mentioned, one tends to think mainly of the American Wild West, but this breed can claim many sources, including origins in the eastern part of the United States. As with the development of so many other breeds, selective crossbreeding was used to develop this particular type. The goal was to produce a smaller, quicker, more compact type of horse, which would be dependable, and which would have a good disposition.

In addition to shining in AHSA Western Division, the Quarter Horse has a multitude of fields in which it excels–or at least holds its

Above: **In addition to the Costume Class, Paso Finos are judged on conformation and performance of the breed's unique and lively gaits.**

Above: **A San Francisco police officer and his Quarter Horse mount on duty in Golden Gate Park.**

Facing page: **A handsome Quarter Horse.**

own—against other breeds. The most notable is racing. It excels in short races of 350-400 yards (320 to 366 meters) in distance, as well as in full quarter-mile races of 440 yards (402 meters), and in doing so has garnered many of the largest purses in American racing! Probably the best known quarter-mile race is the All-American Futurity, which takes place at Ruidoso Downs in New Mexico. Until recently, when the Breeders Cup was inaugurated, it was the country's highest purse, even exceeding that of the Triple Crown races.

The first great Quarter Horse to gain a wide reputation was Steel Dust, foaled in Illinois in 1843 and taken to Lancaster, Texas three years later. Sired by Harry Bluff with his ancestry traced to Sir Archy, he was a blood bay, weighing about 545 kg (1200 pounds). He earned such fame as a racehorse—and as a sire—that his descendants became noted as the best cow horses and running horses. In the following decades, the Steel Dust line of horses became well known throughout the West. The name was quite common until the Ameri-

Above: **Still used by cowboys and ranchers, the adaptable Quarter Horse is also well known as a race horse over short distances.**

can Quarter Horse Association was founded in 1940, and the name 'Quarter Horse' officially adopted.

Another very famous horse of the Quarter Horse line was Peter McCue, foaled in 1895, and owned and bred by Samuel Watkins of Petersburg, Illinois. He was first registered as a Thoroughbred, but it was later proven that his sire was Dan Tucker, who had been sired by Shiloh. Peter McCue stood for service in Texas, western Oklahoma and Colorado, and today, most Quarter Horse lines trace to him. Of the 11,510 Quarter Horses registered before 1948, at least 2304 of them traced their male line to Peter McCue, through his sons, grandsons and great-grandsons. Many of the great Quarter Horse sires have their ancestry traced back to Thoroughbred mares or sires, rather than Quarter Horse. Examinations of the pedigrees reveal that very few of the earlier registrants did not carry some known Thoroughbred breeding close up in their pedigree. As a result, Quarter Horses vary greatly in size, and are therefore bred for a specific type of use, rather than for specific characteristics. Size can range from 386 kg (850 pounds) to as much as 591 kg (1300 pounds), depending upon the purpose for which they are bred.

Quarter Horses are often described in two types: the 'Thoroughbred' type, and the 'Bull Dog' type. The former favors the Thoroughbred in appearance, although it is much more heavily muscled. The

Right: **King Ranch Quarter Commando, a Quarter Horse owned by Australian rancher Bill Trapp.**

Above: **The elegant Saddlebred competes in numerous equestrian events, including under harness.**

latter type has a more chunky conformation and is even more heavily muscled. In early Quarter Horse shows, great emphasis was placed on heaviness of muscling. Since about 1945, however, most winners have been in the middle range.

Likewise, in quarter-mile racing, the Bull Dog type had been considered superior, but now, opinion has swung to favor the Thoroughbred type. As great cutting horses, cow horses and those used in rodeos as dogging and roping horses, many of the Bull Dog type are favored because their great power enables them to quickly reach great speeds over short distances. Good cutting and roping horses generally stop with their hind feet, and can pivot either way, as they tend to keep their legs well under them.

For all rodeo and Western-style events—from team roping to barrel racing to pole bending—Quarter Horses are by far the most popular choice. For the working ranchman or for the youngster with his first mount, they meet the mark in Western riding. At the same time, they do an outstanding job for the outfitter or the dude rancher. Quarter Horse breeders and owners prefer dark or conservative colors in their animals. Off-color animals, such as pinto, appaloosa, or albino, are rejected by the American Quarter Horse Association. Formed in 1940 by a group of breeders in Fort Worth, Texas, today the Association's Quarter Horse Registry is the largest of any breed in the world, with more than two million horses listed.

SADDLEBRED

The elegant Saddlebred epitomizes most people's idea of a show horse, for he moves with a style and grace all his own. The breed was developed on the plantations of Kentucky, Tennessee and Missouri to provide the plantation owners with a comfortable—and cultured—means of transportation. Although this breed was devel-

Above: The Saddlebred is a well-proportioned animal, presenting a beautiful overall picture. The head is well-shaped with large, wide-set expressive eyes and gracefully shaped ears set close together on top of the head. The neck is long and arched, the shoulders deep and sloping.

Facing page: Blazer, a 15-year-old Shetland Pony owned by Barbara Rebok.

oped as a working horse, it is very much at home in the show ring, where it demonstrates its class in either the three-gaited or the five-gaited events. The Three-Gaited Saddlebred produces the three natural gaits—walk, trot, canter—with a high degree of elevation and cadence. The Five-Gaited Saddlebred, which is usually heavier, is trained in two more artificial gaits: a slow gait, a four-beat stepping pace, and a rack, a high speed extended movement in which each foot strikes the ground at equal intervals. These extravagant events are encouraged by the use of heavy shoes and the extreme length of the hooves. Although their cantering movement is more up and down than forward distance, they can be incredibly swift, oftentimes running 1.6 kilometers (one mile) in 2 minutes, 20 seconds. In addition to three-gaited and five-gaited events, the Saddlebred is judged as a harness horse, pleasure horse, park horse, parade horse and roadster.

To achieve the requirements of this breed, the Kentucky breeders used Canadian and Narragansett pacers, crossed with good Morgans, Thoroughbreds and Arabians. The blood of the Thoroughbred, Messenger, used in the development of the Standardbred, also played a major role in the development of the Saddlebred. The Canadian pacer Tom Hall also was considered a great sire in the breed's early days, although the stallion Denmark has been named as the official foundation sire.

The American Saddlebred Horse Association was founded in 1891 and is now located at Lexington, Kentucky. These horses range from bay to black, usually have white markings on their faces and legs and stand between 15 and 16 hands. In spite of their fiery, high-strung appearance, Saddlebred horses are known to have one of the most amiable temperaments, and can be easily ridden or handled by children.

SHETLAND PONY

Standing just 9 to 10.2 hands, this little horse is one of the smallest breeds in the world. Few people fully realize, or appreciate, the value of this little animal, whose ancestors had such a hard life slaving in the mines and on the farms on the stormy Shetland Islands, located 420 kilometers (250 miles) north of northern Scotland and 563 kilometers (350 miles) south of the Arctic Circle. Because it was isolated since the Bronze Age from other breeds of horses except for rare contact with the Icelandic ponies, the Shetland is one of the purest breeds.

Much smaller than even the Welsh Pony, the Shetland is a very strong, rugged breed, which makes it ideal for use as a draft animal in coal mines and on farms. Seldom stabled in the very inclement climate of its native country, the Shetland's heavy coat nevertheless withstood these conditions quite well. When forage was scarce it would eat whatever was available, even seaweed.

The Shetland has long been bred for its pinto (or paint) coloring.

Above: **Rets Reoh Eileen, a Welsh Pony owned and ridden by Krista Head, shows her skill as a jumper at a Mt Vernon, Washington horse show.**

Most commonly, its coat contains white spots on a darker background. The Shetland's small size and gentle disposition has made it a long time favorite. As a riding animal or hitched to a cart, it can be used by people of all ages, even young toddlers. With its patient disposition, the Shetland's value as a child's play partner is priceless. Furthermore, if a child falls from its back, there is little likelihood of an injury as the distance to the ground is relatively small.

After they were brought south to Scotland, these agreeable characteristics became evident, and people began seriously breeding Shetlands. In 1890, the breeders formed the Shetland Pony Stud Book Society and produced Volume I of its stud book the following year. Two years earlier in 1888, the American Shetland Pony Club had been formed, with Buffalo Bill Cody prominent among the 205 breeders listed in the United States. Robert Lilburn owned one of the largest herds in the United States, and registered more than 200 animals in 1906. A total of 425 pedigreed Shetlands were imported from Scotland the same year.

Today, Canada, the Netherlands, Great Britain and parts of South America and Africa have Shetland Pony Clubs. Pony clubs often sponsor informal, local gymkhanas, which feature such events as musical chairs, potato races and obstacle races.

More formal competitions are sponsored by the AHSA. Events include breeding classes as well as performance classes that emphasize the working abilities of this versatile and hardy pony. Shetlands in harness are shown at the park pace and the smart trot; in the roadster class, ponies are shown to a roadster cart as they execute the jog trot, road gait and full trot. Shetlands also compete in classes for pairs and tandems, fancy turnout (viceroy, side-bar buggy, etc), draft harness and under saddle.

WELSH PONY AND COB

Competitions for Welsh Ponies highlight the breed's hardy and spirited temperament. In addition to conformation and breeding classes, ponies compete in formal driving, pleasure classes for both English and Western style, and as roadsters, fine harness ponies, hunters and jumpers, and draft harness ponies. Ponies must not exceed 14.2 hands.

Competitions for Welsh Cobs are divided into two sections: Welsh Pony of Cob Type, for ponies under 13.2 hands, and Welsh Cob for horses over 13.2 hands. Except for size, Welsh Cobs and Welsh Pony of Cob Type are basically identical. These horses are solidly colored, usually a dark hue, and are known to be well-built, intelligent animals. Although there is strong evidence to support the theory that their ancestry goes back to medieval times, after World War II there were only three stallions in existence. Since that time, however, their numbers have blossomed and they have been exported to countries all over the world, including places as far away as Australia.

Above: **The versatile Rets Reoh Eileen, affectionately known as Sahara, performs at a trail competition.**

Overleaf: **A rancher greets his Appaloosa.**

INDEX

Above: **Though no longer a dominant form of transportation, a horse and carriage can sometimes be seen outside the show ring, providing tourists a brief respite from the hectic pace of modern life.**

Photo Credits

Above: **As the day draws to a close, a trainer at the Kentucky Horse Park in Lexington shares a quiet moment with one of his horses.**

Page 96: **After a full day of competing, Jane Lippincott and Tuppence are ready to head for home.**